Praise for *Enough Is Enough*

David has given us a biblically based, psychologically informed, thoroughly researched, practical resource. It is written with wisdom, grace, and a wealth of both clinical and practical experience. This valuable resource provides more than just good information. It will help you reframe how you view your situation, and then give you practical ways to respond rather than merely react. It brings both clarity and comfort in ways that will lead to both healing and hope. I have over fifteen books in my personal library that address abuse, and this is the one that I will recommend.

GARY J. OLIVER, THM, PHD
Executive Director of The Center for Healthy Relationships; Professor of Psychology & Practical Theology at John Brown University; licensed clinical psychologist; author of over 20 books, including *Raising Sons and Loving It*

In my counseling practice, I recurrently recommend *Enough Is Enough* and frequently receive responses thanking me for doing so. *Enough Is Enough* not only empowers abuse victims to put a stop to their abuse, it also provides a clear-cut, instructional path to stopping the abuse. Dr. Clarke's plan of freedom is jam-packed with specific details and directives that pave the way for an abuse-free life. I have witnessed God perform many healing miracles through the information in *Enough Is Enough*. It is a must-read for anyone trapped in an abusive relationship.

LAUREL SLADE-WAGGONER, BCPCC, LMHC, LMFT
Author of *Don't Let Their Crazy Make You Crazy*

Dr. David E. Clarke has done it again! With a direct, blunt, no-nonsense, yet godly style, Dr. David speaks directly to people in abusive relationships who are seeking answers. He does not mince words, and frankly, if you are in an abusive relationship, you don't need someone who will. I love how Dr. David explains the psychology of why people stay in abusive relationships, then provides step-by-step, biblically sound guidance on how to save yourself. I also love that the book is not a "how to divorce your abuser" book. The book gives guidance, yet it offers grace, for those who will accept it. I wholeheartedly recommend this book for those who are in abusive relationships, as well as those who suspect someone they know is in an abusive relationship. I also recommend this book for anyone in a relationship as a way to course correct and self-check. Too many times people offer a myopic view of issues, as they cling either to a purely spiritual or a purely secular perspective. The fact that Dr. David can comfortable meld the two is a treat and offers unimaginable benefits to readers of all Dr. David's works!

REV. KEN J. GORDON JR., PHD
Award-winning author

Enough Is Enough will help you see clearly, act decisively and regain your dignity. Dr. Clarke's no-nonsense approach gives you the best chance to change your situation and save your marriage. It helped save ours!

JASON AND SHELLEY MARTINKUS
Jason is the president of Redemptive Living, a certified coach, and author; Shelley is an author, speaker, and founder of Redemptive Living for Women

Enough *is* Enough

A Step-by-Step Plan to Leave an Abusive Relationship with God's Help

DAVID E. CLARKE, PhD

with WILLIAM G. CLARKE, MA

MOODY PUBLISHERS

CHICAGO

Many of the ideas in chapters 16 and 17 were contributed by Laurel Slade-Waggoner, MS. Used by permission.

Published in association with the Hartline Literary Agency.

Edited by Ginger Kolbaba
Interior design: Ragont Design
Cover design: Erik M. Peterson
Cover illustration of door copyright © 2020 by bagotaj / iStock (1218833196). All rights reserved.

Library of Congress Cataloging-in-Publication Data

Names: Clarke, David, 1959- author. | Clarke, William G., author.
Title: Enough is enough : a step-by-step plan to leave an abusive
  relationship with God's help / David E. Clarke, PhD, with William G.
  Clarke, MA.
Description: Chicago : Moody Publishers, [2021] | Summary: "David Clarke, a
  psychologist specializing in marital therapy, wants to help you find
  refuge from your abusive relationship. You need to get out so you can
  sort it out. Because only with some distance will you be able to see
  what your loving, ever-faithful God has in store for you"-- Provided by
  publisher.
Identifiers: LCCN 2021038717 (print) | LCCN 2021038718 (ebook) | ISBN
  9780802425133 (paperback) | ISBN 9780802476562 (ebook)
Subjects: LCSH: Abused wives--Religious life. | Abused husbands--Religious
  life. | Man-woman relationships--Religious aspects--Christianity. |
  Offenses against the person. | Spousal abuse. | Marriage--Religious
  aspects--Christianity.
Classification: LCC BV4596.A2 C53 2021 (print) | LCC BV4596.A2 (ebook) |
  DDC 261.8/327--dc23
LC record available at https://lccn.loc.gov/2021038717
LC ebook record available at https://lccn.loc.gov/2021038718

Originally delivered by fleets of horse-drawn wagons, the affordable paperbacks from D. L. Moody's publishing house resourced the church and served everyday people. Now, after more than 125 years of publishing and ministry, Moody Publishers' mission remains the same—even if our delivery systems have changed a bit. For more information on other books (and resources) created from a biblical perspective, go to www.moodypublishers.com or write to:

Moody Publishers
820 N. LaSalle Boulevard
Chicago, IL 60610

5 7 9 10 8 6 4

Printed in the United States of America

To all those who have taken the brave, and biblical, step to leave their abusers. May God bless you, your children, and your children's children for having the courage and the faith to get out of an abusive relationship.

Contents

Foreword

A few months ago, my right heel started bothering me. Forget about wearing cute sandals or pretty shoes. I wore my most comfortable tennis shoes, day after day for months.

It seemed like a good solution. I learned to manage the constant ache in my foot. I was doing exercises to strengthen my muscles, so I was attempting recovery. But one evening as I walked barefoot through my house, I realized this was not normal.

What I had been accepting as normal was not healthy and nowhere near ideal. I needed to get help. I decided to call the doctor the next day.

Dear reader, you are holding this book because at some point in your journey, you came to realize that your marriage was not normal, healthy, or anywhere near what marriage promised to be. You've tolerated pain. You've accepted criticism and hurt as normative. You've managed to continue in your responsibilities and your relationship with your children or extended family. But you can't continue much longer in your marriage the way it is. Something has to change.

My experience is writing marriage books like *31 Days to a Happy Husband* and *31 Days to Becoming a Happy Wife.* By no means do I consider myself equipped to address abusive relation-ships. But I know someone who is. My friend Dr. David Clarke has been counseling couples in crisis for more than thirty years. His Bible-based teaching and therapy have guided thousands of hurt-ing men and women toward healthy lives, marriages, and families.

Before you dive into the book, let me warn you: Dr. Clarke is direct. You may even find some of his methods harsh and unortho-dox. This is a good thing! You need someone like Dr. Clarke to open your eyes to new options and possibilities. Give him a chance and hear him out because his ideas really do work. The information in this book comes out of what has worked in his therapy office. This book is intensely practical, giving you a clear road map to follow, which is exactly what you need during this uncertain time in your life.

Maybe you know the Mary Poppins song, "A Spoonful of Sugar." The chorus says that "a spoonful of sugar helps the medicine go down." Humor is a big part of Dr. Clarke's personal life and pro-fessional practice. If you're going to do the hard work of salvaging a broken relationship, it helps to be invited to laugh once in a while. And believe it or not, you will find moments when you will laugh, even as you are reading about this difficult and tender topic.

It's not an accident or coincidence that you have found this book. God is seeking you out because He is so concerned about the hurt you are living with. It's time to get help and healing. What you are experiencing is not normal. But you have a way out, because Jesus is a Way-Maker. You're not alone.

May God bless you in the coming days as you learn how to leave an abusive relationship.

—ARLENE PELLICANE
Speaker, podcast host, and author of *Parents Rising*

It's Time
for Plan B

Y ou had a dream for your life, didn't you? You would find the right person, fall in love, get married, raise a family, and live in an intimate relationship forever. But that dream, that plan A, has not worked out. The beautiful dream has dissolved into sadness, disappointment, frustration, and pain.

You are in a very unhappy marriage, but your situation is much worse than that. From early on in your relationship, your partner has been abusing you. The abusive behaviors don't happen every now and then. They happen regularly. They happen all the time. And these destructive patterns of behavior show no signs of stopping.

The abuse is doing real damage to you and your children.

Many times, you have asked your spouse to change. He won't.

Many times, you have begged him to change. He won't.

Over and over, you have made him aware of your unhappiness and misery because of his treatment of you. He doesn't care.

You have tried everything you can think of to help him stop the abuse: you have loved him unconditionally; you have made the changes he's asked you to make; you have talked to your pastor;

you have talked to a Christian counselor; you have attended marriage seminars; you have read books; you have cried out to God so many times. Nothing has worked. He continues to abuse you.

You have given him countless opportunities to realize he is wounding you deeply and destroying your marriage. He has blown every opportunity. He has no intention of altering his abusive behavior.

You feel like you are out of options. You feel hopeless. You feel helpless. You don't know who to turn to or what to do. And he won't change how he treats you.

WHAT ABUSERS REALLY THINK, SAY, AND DO

The person who was supposed to love you and take care of you has been consistently treating you in one or more abusive ways. Any *one* of these behaviors, taken to an extreme, can be enough to call him abusive. Let's look at what abusers *really* think, say, and do. In each of these categories, I am describing severe abuse.

I Verbally Abuse You

I'm highly critical of you, especially when you don't meet my expectations (and you rarely meet my expectations). I mock you and belittle you for your shortcomings. I attack you personally for your weight, your parenting, your housekeeping, and any area in which you or your actions are unacceptable to me. Sarcasm is my second language.

When you complain, I say "You're too sensitive," "I was just kidding," or "If you'd change, I wouldn't have to criticize you."

I'm going to continue to shred you verbally until there's nothing left of you.

I Neglect Your Needs

The truth is, I'm only aware of my needs. If you would meet my needs, then I would meet yours. Too bad you never fully meet my needs, so you're on your own. It's all about me, and don't forget it. Listen to me and watch my actions.

I'm never going to lift a finger to meet your needs.

I Refuse to Communicate

I don't like to feel vulnerable, so I don't share my feelings or talk with you on a personal level. And I never will. Feel free to share your thoughts and feelings with me, but I will not be listening. If you rattle on too long or press me to open up and talk, I'll end the "conversation" by snapping at you or walking away. I have shut down a million conversations with you.

I'm going to shut down a million more.

I Give You the Silent Treatment

When you do or say something that upsets me, I shut down and ignore you. I also use this technique every time you have the nerve to tell me about a hurt I caused you. When you express an opinion different from mine, I take it as a personal attack. I can stay silent for days and weeks. Even months. I'm punishing you and teaching you never to upset me. I will not allow you to have a voice. My voice, my opinion, is the only one that matters.

I will never talk through any difficult issue with you.

I Control You

I control every area of your life: your contact with your family and friends, where you go, who you spend your time with, how much of my money—and it's all my money—you can spend and what you can spend it on, what clothes you can buy and wear, the church we attend, and how you parent. I have to approve every purchase you make, but I spend my money however I choose. Since I'm a lot smarter than you are, this control makes sense. If you resist, you're not being submissive.

If you stay with me, I will force you to live the way I want you to live for the rest of my life.

I'm Destroying You Financially

I spend too much money. I make bad investments. I don't pay our taxes on time. I'm very secretive about money, and I lie about how I use it. You don't know this, but I'm not saving any money for our retirement. I run up huge debts without telling you. Don't bother working too hard to pay off my debts. Hey, isn't that what bankruptcy is for?

I'll just run up more debts.

I'm a Lazy Slacker

I don't like to work, so I avoid it as much as I can. I go from job to job, and have long stretches of unemployment. For some reason, I can't seem to get along with management. I want you to have a career and shoulder the financial burden for our family. One day—you'll see—I may get a steady job and help support you and the kids. But, then again, probably not. I deserve a great job right now. Why should I work hard to earn it?

I'm so glad I have you to support me for the rest of my life.

I Have Angry Outbursts

My tolerance for frustration is quite low, and often, unpredictably, I blow up. If I'm having a bad day, you're going to have a bad day. I take my stress out on you. I raise my voice, I use profanity, I throw things, and I damage property. I fly into a rage over the smallest, most trivial things. After my outburst of rage, I act as though nothing happened. Or I'll stay angry and cold for days.

I don't think I have an anger problem, so I won't ever get help to fix it.

I'm Violent

When I get angry, I have to hit someone. Since you are the one who usually gets me angry, I hit you. I slap you, punch you, choke you, pin you down, and whatever else I feel like doing in my rage. It isn't my fault I get angry. It's your fault. So don't provoke me, and I won't hit you.

Just so you know, I'm never going to stop hitting you.

I'm an Alcoholic

I love to drink, and I'm not going to stop. It makes me feel good and helps me escape the stresses of life. My drinking makes me mean and verbally abusive, stupid and silly, or completely silent and uninvolved. I hide my drinking, and I lie about it. It ruins just about every party, vacation, and special occasion for us, and many days and weekends in between. Well, it ruins these days for *you.* I'm fine with it. I need the alcohol in order to enjoy myself. I will never admit I'm an alcoholic.

I can stop drinking anytime I want to. I just don't want to.

I'm a Drug Abuser

Even though I'm an adult, I use harmful drugs. They help me cope with stress. They give me a rush. If I don't use harmful drugs, illegal or legal, I am addicted to prescription drugs. My drugs are more important to me than God, you, our kids, and my career.

I'll do the occasional rehab, but I'm not going to stop.

I Have Sexual Issues

I need sex. A lot of sex. So I pressure you for it all the time. I force you to do sexual things you really don't want to do. I don't want or need an emotional or physical connection with you. I just want sex. At times, it will feel like rape to you.

But I don't care. You're not going to do anything about it.

Or I'm on the opposite side of sexual desire, and refuse to be physically intimate with you. You ask for sex, then beg and plead and cry, but I reject you.

I'm going to reject you sexually as long as you stay with me.

I'm a Sexual Sinner

I like porn, and I watch it whenever I can. It's so easy to access, and it's not hurting anyone. Except for you.

And I don't care about you.

I have emotional affairs with coworkers, neighbors, and Facebook "friends." At times, I may also have had physical affairs. Hey, I have sexual needs, and since you won't meet them, what choice do I have? I'm going to continue sinning sexually because it's fun for me. Since you know about my sexual sins and stay with me, I guess you're okay with it.

Like I care.

I Blame You for Everything

It's never my fault. Whenever there's tension or conflict in our relationship, it's your fault. Whenever I'm upset—and I'm upset a lot—it's your fault. I blame others too, but eventually I'll get around to blaming you. Our money problems are your fault. Our marriage problems are your fault. If our kids get into trouble, it's your fault. If you are miserable and depressed, guess whose fault that is?

It's always your fault. And it *will* always be your fault.

ABUSERS DON'T HAVE WARNING LABELS

Of course, abusers don't talk this way. If they did, no one would ever date or marry them. They're all about looking good. And saying these things out loud would not make them look good. But I know abusers, and this is what they think and do.

Abusers can be incredibly charming. They're wonderful in the dating phase of a relationship. They don't show their abusive traits until you've fallen in love with them. Once an abuser has your heart, the abuse begins. And there is a very good chance it will never stop.

I know you wonder if you are in an abusive relationship, or you wonder if someone close to you is. That's why you are reading this book. You bought it or someone gave it to you. Your partner is exhibiting one or more of the characteristics and behaviors in the above list.

You have asked persons close to you—your parents, your siblings, your grandparents, your close friends—about your marriage, and they have told you they believe you are being abused.

You don't know how much more you can take. I'm here to tell you that you don't have to take it anymore.

> *This person who has expressed love for you is acting in a way that is opposite of the Bible's clear, explicit teaching.*

You don't know what to do about the abuse.

I'm going to tell you exactly what to do about the abuse.

You don't have to stay with an abusive partner. This person who has expressed love for you is acting in a way that is opposite of the

Bible's clear, explicit teaching to husbands and is acting in a way that is the opposite of love. "Husbands, love your wives," Ephesians 5:25 teaches, "just as Christ also loved the church and gave Himself up for her" (see also Prov. 31:28; Col. 3:19; 1 Peter 3:7).

It is time to take action.

"Plan A"—or any plan up to now—has not worked.

It's time for plan B.

WHAT IS PLAN B?

I'll cut right to the chase. Plan B is you leaving your abuser. If you have children, you will be taking them when you leave. If you are married, you will not necessarily be divorcing. You can figure that out later. But you will definitely be physically separating.

> *It's time for you to get healthy, fight back, and build a new life.*

This book is a specific, detailed, how-to-leave-your-abuser manual. I'm going to get you ready to leave and show you, step by step, *how* to leave.

My escape plan will take time. You're not leaving tomorrow, or next week, or next month. Depending on your circumstances, it may take up to a year or more before you are ready to leave. But you are leaving.

It's about you now.

This is no longer only about your abuser. This is now also about you. And about your children, if you have children. It's time for you to get healthy, fight back, and build a new life.

Your abuser will have a chance to change and join you in your new life, but only on your terms.

When you are ready, and your support team agrees, you will give your abuser an opportunity to make dramatic changes and win you back. My plan is an effective intervention that will offer your abusive spouse a golden chance to truly repent and work hard to become a godly, loving husband.

I hope and pray your abuser changes. In fact, I've seen abusers change in response to my biblical, tough love, *Enough Is Enough* strategy. But whether your abuser changes or not, my plan will protect you and your children and give you a solid head start on a happy and healthy life.

I CAN HELP YOU GET OUT

I've been a practicing psychologist for more than thirty years. I have a PhD in clinical psychology and a master's degree in biblical studies. I apply God's truth that is found in psychology and God's truth in the Bible, which is ultimate truth. I use both sources in my get-out-of-an-abusive-relationship strategy. I have used my strategy to help hundreds of men and women leave their abusive relationships.

My writing partner (and my dad), William Clarke, has a master's degree in marriage, family, and child therapy. He holds an undergraduate degree in religious education (Bible), and has studied and taught the Bible since he became a Christian at age fifteen. He was a practicing therapist for decades. He understands abusive relationships and has helped many abused persons to escape damaging relationships.

You need a plan that will save you, save your children, and give your abuser the best chance he will ever have to repent and change. My strategy will empower you. It will show you exactly how to leave your abuser. It will protect and improve your physical, emotional, and spiritual health. It will save you and your children from being permanently damaged by your abuser. It will protect your relationship with your children. It will give you a new life free from abuse.

I know my strategy is good for you and your children. No matter what happens to the marriage, you and your kids will be much better off. If I had the room, I could tell you story after story of how this book's plan transformed the lives of abused women.

My strategy also gives your abuser the absolute best shot at breaking patterns of abuse, repenting, and changing. In my experience, not many abusers have changed. But some have. I don't know which abusers will change. You don't know if your abuser will. What I do know is that my plan will give him his chance.

This book does not contain theory. It is *practical truth*. My detailed, specific steps are biblically and psychologically sound.

The plan has six parts:

Part 1: The Definition of Abuse

Knowing the definition of abuse is the beginning of the journey to freedom and happiness. In case you wonder if you are being abused—and I know you do wonder—I make it clear. There has to be a point of beginning, and this is it.

Part 2: Why You Stay

You stay because of your fears. You stay because of the lies you believe. You stay because you think the Bible teaches you to. You stay because your church leaders want you to (maybe the pastor, or a teacher, or a fellow church member).

Part 3: Why You Can Get Out

I would not recommend any strategy if it were not biblical. The good and reassuring news is that leaving an abusive partner is clearly taught in the Bible. God does not want you to stay. He does not want you to go on living in this environment of harm to you and others. I will show you why.

Part 4: How to Get Out

You have to do some hard work in preparation for leaving your abuser. You will have to (1) get spiritually healthy, (2) get a solid support team in place, (3) get emotionally healthy, (4) get financially healthy, (5) get your kids ready to leave, and (6) get to a safe place where you will be living away from your abuser. You will take all these steps in secret. Your abuser will have no idea what you are doing.

Part 5: Give Your Abuser a Chance

When you have left your abuser and are ready for the next step, you will use key members of your support team to confront him and deliver a specific plan for his repentance and change. If he wants you back, he has a lot of work to do in a number of areas. If he doesn't want you back, that has nothing to do with your worth as a child of God. This is his sinful choice.

Part 6: When Your Abuser Does Not Want to Change

What do you do when your abuser refuses to change? In this section, I identify the typical—and very nasty—reactions of the abuser to your departure and your demands of him, and I show you how to respond to him in a healthy, assertive way and move on with your new life.

WONDERING IF THIS BOOK IS FOR YOU?

The plan of action in this book is not for those in an unhappy marriage. My plan is for those who are suffering chronic abuse that is destroying them and their children. If you're in an intimate relationship with an abusive person, this book is for you. Though I write as if you are married, you may be dating or living with an abuser.

You may be a man or a woman. Throughout the book, I refer to the man as the abuser. Yet the woman might also be the abuser. Whether your abusive partner is a man or a woman, my principles remain the same, and my plan will be effective for you.

It's my prayer that you are finally sick and tired of the abuse, of being unhappy, and of living in a relationship that dishonors God. It's time to get righteously *angry*. It's time to do something. It's time to take action to save yourself, your children, and your future.

I'll show you the way out. Let's do this.

PART 1

The Definition of Abuse

CHAPTER 1

The Abuse Never Stops

The woman in her mid-sixties took her seat on my couch. She looked like the perfect grandmother. Gray hair, rosy cheeks, and a nice face. She would have made a great Mrs. Santa Claus.

She was a kind, sweet, and loving person. She told me she had spent her adult life trying to be a good wife, mom, and now, grandma. She doted on her grandchildren. These should have been the best years of her life. They weren't. Every year of the past forty years—ever since she married her husband—had been miserable. Two months after the wedding, he started abusing her. And he'd never stopped.

He criticized her. He belittled her. He called her stupid. He ignored her and her needs. He was somewhat nice only when he wanted sex.

Forty years of abuse.

That's what you're facing unless you decide to do something about it.

You may not be ready to admit you are in an abusive relationship. It's not easy to let go of the dream of a happy relationship

> *Abuse is a pattern of narcissistic, disrespectful, and harmful behavior exhibited by one person in an intimate relationship.*

with a loving partner. You've coped for a long time by living in denial. You love this man and choose to believe he loves you.

You cling to the hope that one day he will change, and you will have a healthy, intimate relationship.

I'm going to communicate with you the same way I do with my abused clients in my therapy office. I'm going to show you the brutal truth about your man. I'm going to push you past denial and into reality. When you finish reading the chapters in this first section, you won't wonder if you have an abusive partner, you'll *know* whether you do or not.

So we're on the same page, here is how I define abuse: *Abuse is a pattern of narcissistic, disrespectful, and harmful behavior exhibited by one person in an intimate relationship.*

In this part's chapters (1–5), we're going to take a closer look at each of the elements in this definition as I build a profile of your abuser. Let's start with the first element—that abuse is a pattern.

ABUSE IS A PATTERN

I'm not talking about one or two incidents of abusive behavior.

I'm not talking about a decent, loving spouse who is guilty of the occasional insensitive word or action.

I'm not talking about a man who has seriously sinned, but has confessed, repented, is in recovery, and has helped you heal from what he did to you.

I'm not talking about someone who has admitted his weaknesses as a husband, owns the blame for wounding you, and is in the process of changing.

I'm not talking about someone who is seeing your pastor or a Christian counselor—alone or with you—and is working hard to improve as a spouse.

I'm not talking about a spouse who has been very selfish, but is now sincerely trying to learn how to identify and meet your needs.

I am talking about a person who abuses you on a regular basis. He started abusing you early in your relationship, and he has continued to abuse you. He may say he wants to stop. He may even shed tears and say how sorry he is for hurting you. It's an act because he doesn't stop the abuse.

His words mean nothing. His behavior means everything. He is not going to stop abusing you.

He actually enjoys saying and doing things that make you miserable. It's what he does. It's who he is.

Remember the list of "What Abusers Really Think, Say, and Do" I covered in the introduction (page 12)? In whichever categories your abuser fits, he consistently abuses you in these ways over and over and over. Week after week after week. Month after month after month. Year after year after year.

The abuse never stops. It's not going to stop until you take action.

HE HAS NO LEARNING CURVE

To this date, your abuser has never been truly repentant. That's because he's not sorry for any of his abusive behaviors. He'll occasionally say the words *I'm sorry*, but they are only words. He says them only to stop the conversation and get you off his back.

Because he does not feel genuine remorse, he does not change. He has no learning curve. He thinks your pain is your problem, not his. He reasons that it's not his fault you're in pain, it's your fault.

So if anybody has to change, he believes it's you. You, you, you.

When you complain to him about his behavior, it's worse than a waste of time. His responses to your pain cause you more pain:

"You're too sensitive."

"You misinterpreted what I said."

"You're making a mountain out of a molehill."

"You're only crying to manipulate me."

"You're making it all up in your head."

"You are way too emotional."

"You won't forgive me."

"You're attacking me."

When you ask him to go with you to a counselor, here's what he says:

"Counseling is a waste of time and money."

"Counseling won't help, because you won't change."

"I've already gone to counseling."

"You are never satisfied. You always want to go to another counselor."

"If you're that unhappy, counseling won't do any good. Just leave."

"You know you don't love me. No amount of counseling will make you love me."

"Why should I try when you do absolutely nothing for the marriage?"

"Counseling is one more way you try to control me."

He doesn't think his treatment of you is abuse, so in his mind it isn't. You have no right to be upset. When you are upset, it's your fault. When you have the nerve to bring up something negative about him, he actually thinks you are abusing him.

His thinking is irrational, wrong, abnormal, and sinful. Normal persons can take responsibility for their actions. He can't and won't do that. He has no learning curve.

Yet you continue to try to help him change.

THE PATTERN IS ENTRENCHED

This abusive pattern is entrenched. You know that, because you've tried every conceivable way to change your abuser and your marriage.

You've been patient.

You've been kind.

You've unconditionally loved him.

You've met his needs.

You've served him faithfully.

You've bitten your tongue a million times when he has hurt you.

You've brought up your concerns to him repeatedly.

You've cried in front of him.

You've begged him to change.

You've dragged him to your pastor.

What is the result of all of your efforts? I know the answer. No change.

You've dragged him to counselors.

You've dragged him to marriage seminars.

You've read scores of books on marriage.

You've tried to be the best wife you possibly could be.

You've prayed your heart out countless times.

Let me ask you a dumb but important question: What is the result of all of your efforts? I know the answer. No change. Same old abuse. Same old abuser.

You wouldn't be reading this book if any of these strategies had worked.

If you haven't tried counseling with a Christian, experienced, licensed therapist, give that a shot. If your spouse is willing to go and to genuinely work hard, counseling can help him break his abusive pattern. If your spouse refuses to go or goes once or twice and then quits, you know that the tough love plan in this book is for you.

Without an effective intervention, your husband is going to be an abuser the rest of his life. The good news is, you don't have to take his abuse the rest of *your* life.

You don't have to continue to tolerate his pattern of destructive behavior. My plan is the best choice for you and your children. It will protect you, get you away from the abuse, and lead to a new and better life. My plan is also *your husband's* best chance for change.

CHAPTER 2

World-Class Selfishness

I had my first session with the successful businessman and his wife. How successful was he? Well, if I had given him six hours, he would have spent the entire time telling me just how prosperous he was.

From the moment his successful rear end hit my couch, the session was all about him. His superb education. His amazing career results. His incredibly fit body. His impressive charity work. His massive income.

I asked some strategic questions about his childhood, which revealed that his fawning parents had groomed him to be selfish. He was the favorite child—the special one. He could do no wrong from the moment of his birth. All his achievements were magnified and celebrated.

He married his sweet wife only because she was attractive and seemed willing to keep him on his pedestal of glory. He was the big fish. She was the pilotfish whose job was to idolize him and devote her life to his service.

He expected her to raise the kids, take care of the home, handle his laundry, cook for him, have sex on demand, and do everything needed to advance his career. If he was happy, he figured she should be happy.

They came to me because Mister Perfect's affair had just been revealed. He made it clear that he wasn't sorry. Furthermore, he said his adultery was 100 percent his wife's fault because she hadn't met his needs.

Not all abusers are narcissists. But most are.

When I told him his adultery was 100 percent his fault, he got angry. When I told him he had been a lousy, abusive husband for years, he had a fit and walked out of my office. It may have been the first time anyone had possessed the nerve to tell him he was wrong about something.

After he slammed my office door, I said to his wife, "I thought he'd never leave. Let's work on helping you heal from his adultery and all the other wounds he's inflicted on you. And with God's help, I'll get you strong enough to leave him. Once you are out, he'll have his opportunity to change and get you back."

Let's look back at our definition of abuse: *it is a pattern of narcissistic . . . behavior.*

Not all abusers are narcissists. But most are. Even if your spouse doesn't get a diagnosis of narcissistic personality disorder, his incredible selfishness is a key part of his abusive behavior.

"IT'S ALL ABOUT ME, BABY"

A narcissist is a spectacularly selfish individual. Super-selfish, world-class selfish. Everything he thinks, feels, and does focuses on one goal—to protect and please himself. The truth is, abused wife, your husband doesn't love you. He has feelings for you, particularly when you are meeting his needs. But he is incapable of loving anyone but himself. He lives in a universe of one. He is only aware of what *he* thinks. What *he* feels. What *he* needs. What *he* wants to do.

What you think, feel, need, and want to do doesn't matter. You're not even on his radar screen.

Your abuser lives in his own reality. Whatever he thinks is accurate. Always. You must agree with him, or you'll pay the price.

He lies continually, but he never admits any of his lies. He doesn't think he's lying. He believes his own lies, so he's very persuasive. He can even convince you of something that you know isn't true!

His life's mission is I, I, I . . . me, me, me . . . my, my, my.

It is always and forever about him.

He's always the smartest and best-looking person in the room. He craves attention and approval and has to be in the limelight. He is convinced that you should spend every waking minute being unbelievably grateful that you are married to him.

He is condescending because he believes he's better than everyone else. He has to bear the burden of never being wrong. This means, of course, that *you* are always wrong. Every decision he makes is based on what will make him look good, what will make him happy, and what is best for him.

"WHAT DO YOU MEAN, YOUR NEEDS?"

This man will not meet your needs. As far as he is concerned, you don't have any needs. When he does something nice for you, it's for the purpose of getting something from you. To him, the only reason for your existence is to meet his needs. You're supposed to worship him. Adore him. Support him. Praise him. Do whatever it takes to make him happy. He believes you are incredibly lucky to have the job of meeting his needs. It's a wonderful privilege for you—a privilege that, in his mind, quite frankly, you don't deserve. If you ever have the gall and poor taste to question his love for you, he'll immediately shut down or launch into a long rant listing all the things he has done for you, starting with marrying you.

Not all these descriptions of narcissism fit your abuser, but I'll bet many do. Living with a man this selfish is bad and painful and joy-robbing. And it always will be.

CHAPTER 3

Less-than-Zero Respect

I stared in awe at the abuser sitting on my couch. He had just put on a performance worthy of an Oscar.

His wife had spent twenty minutes describing a dozen experiences in which he had abused her in the past ten years. I know she could have easily included many more abusive events, but my sessions are limited to forty-five minutes. She talked about neglect, verbal abuse, and several episodes of physical abuse. Her description of each occurrence was rich with detail, including specific times and places. As she spoke, her emotions flowed.

I believed her.

When she finished and was crying softly, I asked the abuser, "Well, what do you say?"

With a straight face and just the right amount of humility, he replied: "Doc, I have no memory of any of these events. I don't remember a single one."

I wanted to yell, "Liar!" I didn't. I don't waste my breath and time on liars. When I saw his wife the next week in an individual session, she told me she was worried she was losing her mind. In addition to her husband denying any abuse, she was losing things. In the past few months, she had lost her watch, several pieces of jewelry, and her Bible. These articles later turned up in the strangest places.

"Your husband is lying his head off," I told her. "He remembers every one of these abusive events. Why would his memory be accurate for everything except the times he abused you? And he's the one hiding your stuff and moving it around."

Her eyes grew wide in surprise.

"There's nothing wrong with you," I continued. "You are sharp and articulate, and your memory is fine. What's wrong is this: you have a husband who's trying to drive you crazy. If he can prove to others that you're nuts, no one will believe you when you speak of his abuse. I have a strategy that will restore your confidence and drive *him* crazy. We'll see how he likes it."

> His disrespect for you is intended to dismantle your identity.

In our definition of abuse, we see that it is *a pattern of . . . disrespectful behavior.*

Your abuser is disrespectful to you. He continually crosses the line to mistreat you. Over and over again.

It is less-than-zero respect, because his treatment of you goes beyond a simple absence of respect. Disrespecting you is a way of life for him.

His disrespect is not minor and accidental. It's outrageous and deliberate. He disrespects you in order to marginalize you, to make you believe that what you think and feel is wrong, distorted, irrational, and irrelevant.

He is depersonalizing you. His disrespect for you is intended to dismantle your identity. He is tearing apart who you are—as a person, as a wife, as a friend, as a Christian—piece by piece. *And you feel it happening.*

PROFESSIONAL "GASLIGHTING"

The husband in the above story was using a particularly nasty and extreme form of disrespect—he was gaslighting. Gaslighting is an intentional campaign your spouse is using to make you doubt yourself and what you're thinking and feeling. It's supposed to destroy your self-confidence and make you doubt your abilities. He acts in ways that keep you confused, off-balance, and dependent. He is, quite literally, trying to drive you crazy.

The abuser wants you—and others—to doubt your sanity. He's deliberately attacking your credibility. This keeps him in a superior position, in control, and compromises your relationship with your children and others in your social circle.

He's building a narrative that proves you're crazy and unstable and untrustworthy. The result is no one will believe you, and you'll be seen as the problem. Plus, by communicating this false message, he scores major martyr points when he tells others: "I'm doing my best to live with this unstable, lying, mixed-up woman."

He keeps up regular attacks on your memory. When you say something happened, all he has to do is deny it:

"I didn't say that."
"I didn't do that."
"I didn't promise that."
"You didn't say that."
"You didn't do that."
"I don't remember that."

"That's not what happened."
"You don't know what you're talking about."

He does not respect what you say and think and feel and remember. Worse than that, he denies your thoughts, feelings, and memories. You are portrayed as crazy or a liar. Or both.

OPPOSITE WORLD

Your abuser will deliberately do or say something to provoke you. This bolsters his narrative that you are the one with the problems. He wants you to be upset and angry so he can blame you for the conflict. He'll often provoke you in front of the children and others so they will see you in a negative light. He hopes others will conclude:

"Look at her, all angry over something trivial."
"She's out of control."
"She's unstable."
"She's crazy."
"She's unreasonable."
"She's way too emotional."
"She has huge mood shifts."
"She has an anger problem."
"She's hysterical."
"She's a drama queen."

With your abuser, it's what I call "opposite world." All the actions he's guilty of are projected onto you. He wants you to think that *he* isn't guilty of these abusive behaviors, *you* are! When you have the nerve to call him on something, he turns it immediately back on you:

"I'm not the liar, you're a liar."

"I didn't do that, you did."

"I wasn't angry, you were angry."

"I'm not a control freak, you are."

"I'm not abusive, you are."

NO CONSCIENCE, NO EMPATHY

Two other options on his menu of dysfunctional, disrespectful responses to the truth are silence and personal attacks. When you bring up an issue he doesn't want to deal with—which is just about any issue—he may have no response. Complete silence. It's as if you never spoke at all. Or he will launch into a personal attack on you, completely ignoring the issue you raised. He'll go on a rant criticizing you. He'll belittle you. He'll be bitingly sarcastic. He'll mock you. He'll describe things you've done to hurt him.

He may say he's sorry, but those are only words.

His lack of a conscience is what drives his disrespectful behavior. He doesn't feel guilt or shame when he hurts you. Or, if he does feel anything, it doesn't stop his abusive behavior. Saying "I'm sorry" is easy. Changing behavior is hard. He may say he's sorry, but those are only words. He can fake "sorry," but he can't actually *be* sorry.

Again, go on his behavior, not his words.

He has no empathy. He has no capacity for compassion. He could not care less about your feelings. When he says or does something that deeply hurts you, he won't allow you to vent those feelings of pain on him. He'll say, "I said I was sorry. Let it go. You need to forgive me so we can move on."

He focuses on your "lack of forgiveness," not his damaging behavior that caused the problem in the first place. If he admits guilt for his negative behavior, he often will say that it was your fault anyway.

Just as with the other categories of abuse, here too nothing is ever his fault; it's always someone else's fault. Perfect persons don't make mistakes, and he believes he's perfect. The very idea of changing is ludicrous because someone who's perfect doesn't need to change.

He believes you are the one who's wrong; you're the one who needs to change. He expects you to keep trying to be the best wife you can be, and he will try to tolerate your supposed shortcomings.

In his view, you'll never be good enough. That's how the game is played.

He intensely rejects any criticism of himself because he cannot allow his vision of personal superiority to be tarnished in the slightest way. If you're critical, he'll become angry, whining, "You're beating me up."

He's strongly critical of you in just about every area. He criticizes you in order to "help you become a better person." If you don't meekly accept his criticism, he'll criticize you for that, too.

"IT'S MY WAY"

He makes decisions without consulting you. Since he's never wrong, and he wants to do what he wants to do without interference, your input is not necessary. He will graciously inform you of his decisions and expect your unconditional approval.

For example, he makes money and spends it the way he wants to spend it. If you make the money, he'll still spend it the way he wants to spend it. You, however, must get his permission to spend money on things you want.

He manipulates you and others to get his way. Getting his way is all that counts. How he gets his way isn't important. If he has to lie to get what he wants, he'll lie. He is a *very* good liar. What's worse, he believes his lies.

His relentless, damaging disrespect for you knows no bounds. He's systematically stripping you of your respect for yourself, of your sense of self-worth. He is also taking away the respect others—the most important persons in your life—have for you: your children, your family, your friends, your coworkers, your neighbors, and your church leaders.

You don't have to keep living with this abuse. It's time to get your respect back.

CHAPTER 4

A Slow, Painful Death

It was my first session with a wife who had been living with an abusive husband for twenty years. She came alone because he had no interest in "wasting time and money on some psychologist quack."

As is the case with many of my clients, she had come to me as a last resort. She told me she was miserable, under a huge load of stress, and felt hopeless. She'd heard about my "aggressive, *tough love* approach" and wanted to know if it fit her situation.

Because of the abuse her husband dished out on a regular basis, she was experiencing pain and deterioration in every area of her life.

Physically, she was a wreck. She was exhausted most of the time. She had frequent headaches, stomach problems, and a compromised immune system. Her doctors couldn't find a reason for her physical symptoms.

I told her I knew exactly the reason for her physical symptoms.

Emotionally, she was a wreck. She couldn't sleep well, was depressed, and felt anxious much of the time. She'd had a few panic attacks, which terrified her. Her self-esteem was just about nonexistent.

Her previous counselors couldn't find a psychological cause for all her emotional symptoms. I told her I knew exactly the source of her psychological symptoms.

Spiritually, she was a wreck as well. She still loved God but felt increasingly distant from Him. Her prayers, her Bible reading, and her quiet times with God all had become empty and frustrating and were not bringing her the peace she had experienced in the past. She was far from a joyful, peace-filled Christian.

Her pastor couldn't find a spiritual reason for her problems with God. I told her I knew exactly the reason for her spiritual symptoms.

I told her what she already knew deep inside, but didn't want to admit to herself. Her abusive husband was causing her breakdown in these three areas. She was suffering a slow, painful death. I told her that when she got away from the abuse, she would regain her physical, emotional, and spiritual health.

In a pleading voice, my client said to me: "But I want to save my marriage! I don't want a divorce. I want a better marriage!"

In words I use with all my clients, I told her: "I agree with you. I don't want you to get a divorce either. You will never hear me recommend divorce. But you need to save yourself before you can save your marriage.

The abuse is not only blocking any joy in your life, it's destroying you—you, who were created in God's image and are loved by Him.

"You're too weak and sick now to take any constructive steps in any major area of your life. As you grow healthier and stronger as a person, you will be able to follow my plan of action. My plan gives you the best chance to save and improve your marriage.

"But my plan starts with you. At this point, I wouldn't work with your husband even if he wanted to come in and talk with me. The first step of my recovery plan is about you and regaining your identity and your health. Once you're where you need to be, then we'll focus on the marriage."

As we continue to look at our definition of abuse, we see it is *a pattern of . . . harmful behavior.*

Your abuser's behavior is doing you harm—serious, debilitating harm. You've learned to live with it. But the abuse is not only blocking any joy in your life, it's destroying you—you, who were created in God's image (Gen. 1:26) and are loved by Him (John 3:16, Rom. 5:8). It's a form of never-ending torture. And the stress from it is very real.

ABUSE STRESS

We all deal with stress. It is a normal part of life. The stress of living with an abuser is not normal. It's abnormal. It's constant. It's severe. It's damaging.

All the clients I work with (in person or by telephone or email) who live with an abuser tell me they are not doing a good job in any area of their lives. They're having trouble at work. They're having difficulty raising their kids and being the loving moms they want to be. They're not as close to their friends. They're feeling distant and awkward with their families. They are struggling to serve God in their church. The effects of disrespect and even disdain—as opposed to love and praise—stain their lives like ink in a glass of water.

My response to these clients' terrible strain and unhappiness is: "I believe you. You aren't able to do a good job in any of these areas. The stress of living with your abuser is taking a toll on you across the board. No part of your life escapes the impact of his abuse."

Of course, your abuser feels fine. He feels no pain. He sleeps soundly at night. His physical health isn't affected by your lousy marriage. Spiritually, he's actually a mess, but he would never believe that.

When you don't have the capacity to truly care about someone else, nothing that happens to that person bothers you. He doesn't care that you're miserable and lonely and breaking down. He believes that it's your problem, that it's all in your head, that it's your fault.

YOU'RE LOSING YOURSELF

You are being broken down day by day, month by month, year by year—physically, emotionally, and spiritually. You will reach the point, if you have not already, where you don't recognize yourself anymore.

You're allowing him to rip from you your self-worth—your identity, your sense of value as a person, your feelings of dignity. Soon there will be nothing left of you.

You're not living; you are surviving—barely.

Here's what one woman told me about the abuse she has lived with in her marriage:

We've been married twenty years. It took me fifteen years to figure out that my husband was an abuser. I didn't want to see that or believe it. It took another five years to completely grasp and accept his unwillingness even to acknowledge his treatment of me and to change. I spent years suppressing his painful words and actions, trying to forget many of the nasty things he'd done to me and our kids.

This relationship has cost me everything. I am at a point now where I would rather not live than wake up one more day living in fear, isolation, and misery. I feel like I'm trapped in a prison. The pain is so consuming and overwhelming. I can't see how my heart can bear any more pain.

I have surrendered my life for him. I gave up my dreams for him to pursue his needs and desires. I don't know who I am anymore. I'm not the person I once was.

Don't lose yourself. Every woman I've helped escape from her abuser has said these same things to me:

I feel so much better. I didn't realize how sick I was until I left him. I am regaining my physical health. I have a lot more energy now. I am actually happy for the first time in a long time. I'm close to God, which is so important to me. I feel like I've gotten myself back. I can see a bright future now.

This was a rough chapter, wasn't it? It isn't easy to realize all the awful damage your abuser is inflicting on you. It's hard to accept that this abuse is causing you to die a slow, painful death.

CHAPTER 5

Much Worse than an Unhappy Marriage

The woman sat in my office and confessed the truth about her marriage:

> Dr. Clarke, it hurts so badly because it's my husband doing these things to me. I've given my life to him. And my future. We have children together. I love him.
>
> I want desperately for my marriage to work and for us to be close.
>
> He can be great at times. Loving, caring, generous. Even romantic. But only at times. Unpredictably, he'll switch and turn into the abusive person.
>
> Everyone outside our home loves him and thinks he's a wonderful person. They don't see what I see. They don't know him as I know him.
>
> So many times, he'll start to change. He'll be nicer. He'll do and say things that make me think maybe he's

finally "got it." But he always quits and goes back to his old, abusive, cruel self. My hopes are crushed.

I want intimacy so badly, but we've never really had it. Not on any consistent basis. Even in the good times, and there aren't many, we're not connected on a deep level. His abuse kills any chance for real intimacy.

I'm not just unhappy, although I'm unhappy in this marriage. It's worse than that. I'm miserable.

I'm in pain most of the time. It's a special form of torture. It's an awful way to live. I have to admit that what I'm doing isn't working. I don't know what to do, but I have to do something different. That's why I came to you.

Before we talk about why you stay with this abusive person and why you should leave, let's focus on the last part of my definition of abuse: Abuse is a pattern of narcissistic, disrespectful, and harmful behavior *exhibited by one person in an intimate relationship.*

Your abuser is intentionally preventing any possibility of intimacy. Your abuser is forcing you to experience the opposite of intimacy. The loss of intimacy is just as painful as the abusive behavior that causes it.

Let's look again at the woman's story above and break it down to see how abusers crush intimacy.

HE HURTS YOU MORE THAN ANYONE ELSE DOES

Abuse does the greatest damage in what began as a romantic/ loving relationship. When you love someone and consider him to be the most important person in your life, he can hurt you as no one else can.

Because you desperately want your relationship to work, and

you are the only one trying to make it work, you're vulnerable and wide open for hurt. Your weaknesses and soft spots are completely exposed to him. He knows exactly how to make you hurt, and that is what he does—over and over.

HE'S LOVING AT TIMES

Your abuser has his moments when he can be nice to you. This is usually because he's having a good day or because he wants something from you. And when I say moments, I mean moments. He's not nice for long.

We find a description of real, true, genuine, God-inspired love in 1 Corinthians 13:4–8. This beautiful, moving Bible passage describes the kind of love every woman (in fact, every human!) wants and needs. The problem is, your abuser exhibits behavior that is opposite of the qualities of love in this passage:

First Corinthians 13:4–8 Versus Your Abuser's Behavior

Love is patient. He's impatient with you.

Love is kind. He's mean to you.

Love is not jealous. He's jealous of your time and attention that's not devoted to him.

Love does not brag, and is not arrogant. He's prideful.

Love does not act unbecomingly. His behavior is unbecoming.

Love does not seek its own. He's always seeking his own interests.

Love is not provoked. He's provoked very easily.

Love does not take into account a wrong suffered. He takes into account every wrong he thinks he's suffered.

Love does not rejoice in unrighteousness. He enjoys making you suffer.

Love rejoices with the truth. He wouldn't know the truth if it slapped him in the face.

Love bears all things. He bears nothing; everything upsets him.
Love believes all things. He believes only in himself.
Love hopes all things. He hopes only to get his needs met.
Love endures all things. He endures nothing.
Love never fails. His "love" fails all the time.

OTHERS LOVE HIM

Typically, your abuser does not show his narcissism, disrespect, and harmful behavior in public. He's too smart for that. It's important to him to look like an awesome person to others. What others think about him is much more important to him than what you think about him.

He's charming and charismatic and caring in social environments. Your church leaders, your church friends, your extended family, and your friends and neighbors all think he's the greatest guy in the world.

He can be very generous with his time and energy and money with others. He won't do squat for you, but he'll drop everything and run and help someone else.

When you leave him, you'll lose the popularity contest. But you will win back your life.

The world at large admires him. Behind closed doors in your home, he's a very different person.

When you're ready to begin telling others the truth about him, many will not believe you. They'll think you're lying, crazy, or both. You'll be the complaining one, the bad guy. They'll believe him and his lies and the image he has projected.

When you leave him, you'll lose the popularity contest. But you will win back your life.

HE'LL START TO CHANGE, BUT THEN . . .

At times, he will act as if he's working on your relationship. He'll go to a counselor with you. He'll talk to your pastor. He'll attend a Bible study or a marriage seminar. He actually has no intention of changing. He believes he doesn't need to change; you do. He's only humoring you and does it to look good to the kids and others. It fits his narrative that he's a great person, a great husband, and he's doing his best for the marriage. All he's doing by these actions is showing others he's "trying." These efforts are part of his public relations campaign. He'll say to others, "I tried . . . I did this . . . I did that," and describe his "meritorious" actions. "Here's a list of all I have done to work on my marriage," he'll say. "I'm doing my best, but it's never enough for her."

LOVE FOR YOU IS NOT ON HIS AGENDA

There is no real love and intimacy with an abuser. He loves himself, not you. He wants to get his needs met; he wants you to cook, clean, take care of the kids, and give him sex; he wants to stay in control; and he wants to look good to others.

Most of the time he's not thinking divorce, but it's not because he loves you. It's because divorce is losing. Divorce is expensive. Divorce will make him look bad.

IT'S NOT ONLY UNHAPPINESS,
IT'S MISERY AND ABUSE

What you're going through is much, much worse than just an unhappy marriage. I have written other books for those in an unhappy marriage. This book is for a person who is living with chronic, debilitating abuse—abuse that is shredding you and your children to little pieces.

Don't use this book as an excuse to leave an unhappy marriage. Your reason to escape must be legitimate, continual abuse—the abuse I've described in the introduction and past five chapters.

DO YOU GET IT?

Though not every trait I've covered may fit your abuser, I'll bet my profile is pretty close to what you are dealing with in your relationship. So have I convinced you that your man is an abuser, that you *are* experiencing abuse? If I have, good. If I haven't, keep reading.

It's a hard and painful truth, but the sooner you believe it, the sooner you can start the process of getting away from the abuse.

PART 2

Why
You
Stay

CHAPTER 6

"But I Don't Want to Leave"

I've worked with hundreds and hundreds of abused women over the past thirty years. Once I clearly establish that they are being abused, I always recommend they start my leaving-the-abuser process.

With few exceptions, these women resist the idea of leaving. *Resist* doesn't adequately describe their reaction. They fight tooth and nail.

Why do they fight so hard to stay with these persons who once pledged their love to them and now treat them so hatefully? One of the main reasons is fear. Their fear of leaving the abuser is deep and powerful and extends to many areas.

Until they overcome their fear, they won't leave.

DIALOGUE WITH AN ABUSED WOMAN

Here's a dialogue I had with an abused woman. In it, you'll see many of the classic fears of women in abusive relationships. You will also see my responses to each one.

ABUSED: I fear I'll never be strong enough to leave him.

DAVE: I know you're not strong enough . . . yet. You can't do it alone, anyway. You will have a solid support team. Ultimately, God can give you the strength. Philippians 4:13 says: "I can do all things through Him who strengthens me." "All things" includes leaving your abuser.

> By leaving your abuser, you are actually being a good wife and mother.

ABUSED: I'm scared of quitting. Leaving feels like quitting.

DAVE: I'm urging you to quit doing what you've been doing because it's not working. You're not going to stop trying. You're going to try a different strategy, one that has a chance of producing a much better husband and marriage.

ABUSED: I fear that, by leaving, I won't be acting like a good wife and mother.

DAVE: Like most women, you are kind, nice, and caring. By nature, you are a nurturer. You continue to nurture even when you're being abused. If nurturing were going to work, it would have worked with your abuser by now. It's like having a bad dog that bites you on a regular basis. When you try to feed it, it bites you. When you try to pet it, it bites you. When you're doing nothing at all, it bites you. You need to get away from the dog. By leaving your abuser, you are actually being a good wife and mother. You are nurturing your kids and protecting them. And you are giving your abuser a golden opportunity to change into a godly example of a good man, mate, father, friend, and follower of Christ.

ABUSED: I fear that if I leave, there's no hope for the marriage. I guarantee he'll never forgive me for walking out. I would be responsible for that.

DAVE: The hope you're clinging to is a form of denial. Staying and tolerating and enduring his abuse and hoping he'll change will just keep you from dealing with the awful reality of your situation and thus will keep it the same. Leaving him is the only hope for your marriage. He'll either finally break and get help to save his marriage, or he will continue being an abuser. If he blames your leaving for the end of the marriage, that's your answer. He'll never change. The right man, the man who loves God and his wife and his children, will always do whatever it takes to win his wife back. The wrong man won't.

ABUSED: I fear being alone.

DAVE: That's spoken like a true codependent person, but you're alone now even in this relationship, and you don't realize it. You don't think you can make it without him, do you? Your abuser intentionally works to keep you dependent on him. He keeps you confused, off-balance, and emotionally upset. He attacks your self-esteem and undermines your confidence in yourself. He wants to believe that you can't make it on your own. This is what he wants you to believe. I'm telling you, you *can* make it on your own. Even if you end up living alone, you're better off than living with an abuser. But you won't be alone. You'll build a new life with people who love you.

ABUSED: I fear I'll lose my kids if I leave him.

DAVE: By staying this long, you are already in the process
of losing your kids. If you stay, you lose your children for
sure because of the effect the abuse will have on them.

ABUSED: I fear that leaving isn't best for my children.

DAVE: I want you to believe that leaving *is* best for your
children. I could spend hours and hours telling you sto-
ries of moms who chose to stay with the abuser and who
watched their kids suffer well into adulthood because
of that choice. Here's what happens to your kids if you
stay: They are deeply wounded by watching the abuse;
they lose respect and love for you. They will also abuse
you because they saw their father do it; therefore, it is
right, you deserved it. They side with Dad because he's a
wonderful liar and is the stronger parent. And they don't
see much of the abuse. Statistics show that it's very likely
your boys will become abusers and your girls will marry
abusers. Plus, your kids will blame you for staying and not
protecting them. And they'll be right! If you won't leave
for yourself, leave for the sake of your children.

ABUSED: I fear what will happen when my children must
interact with women my husband may date and possibly
marry.

DAVE: You can't control that. God will protect your kids. It's
far better for them to stop watching Dad abusing Mom.
And less time with an abusive father is better for them.

ABUSED: I fear losing my dream of having a happy marriage
and a happy, healthy family.

DAVE: I know that dream is the desire of your heart. But you have to let it go. You have to grieve the loss of the dream, at least the way you have been pursuing it. That's brutally hard and painful, and very sad. But it's necessary if you are to follow my plan of escape. You need a new dream, one that may or may not include your abuser. He'll have to change to be a part of your new dream.

ABUSED: I fear that leaving is not biblical and my church leaders will not support it.

DAVE: I know you want to honor God and do what He wants you to do. I want that too. I would never recommend any plan of action not supported in Scripture. I will show you how my plan of escape is biblical. And I will dismantle the flawed arguments of church leaders who believe you should stay with your abuser.

If you do have any anything to fear, it's ultimately this: If you stay, you are guaranteed misery and destruction. Don't let your fears prevent you from leaving your abuser.

CHAPTER 7

"My Church Threw Me under the Bus"

The wife sat on my office couch, slumped forward, and started to cry. When she was able to talk, she told me a story I have heard many times from abused wives. She told me what her pastor had done when she went to him for help with her abusive husband:

In our first meeting, I talked with my pastor alone. I told him about the abuse I had suffered for years. After talking about the importance of marriage and reading a few verses about love, he told me to stay in the home, submit to my husband, and keep on loving him and meeting his needs.

My husband and I both went to the second meeting with our pastor. My husband put on quite a convincing performance, admitting in a general way to some mistakes and saying he was sorry. To my shock, my pastor gave my husband a pass! He said since my husband had apologized, I had to forgive him and move on.

My pastor told me that my husband's behavior was partly my fault. He told me that if I would be a better wife, my husband would treat me better. He gave us a book on communication and said he'd pray for us.

Dr. Clarke, I can't believe my pastor didn't confront my husband about his abuse of me! He talked more about things I was doing wrong! Far from helping me, he actually made my situation worse.

I felt like my church threw me under the bus. My church won't support or help me. I feel totally alone. What do I do now?

Too many local church leaders—pastors, elders, deacons, small group leaders, Bible teachers, men's and women's ministry leaders, lay counselors, and church-based counselors—have no idea how to deal with a marriage in which abuse occurs. They give the wrong advice and end up doing more damage to the abused spouse.

Once leaders listen to each spouse and are able to establish that abuse is taking place in the marriage, these leaders have a responsibility to comfort, protect, and defend the abused spouse. Instead, they often comfort, protect, and defend the abusive spouse. These leaders are called to confront the abusive spouse and require him to acknowledge his sin, repent, and change. Instead, they often confront the abused spouse and require her to repent and change.

Are these church leaders godly persons? Most often, yes. Are they well-meaning? Yes. Are they misunderstanding and misusing Scripture? Yes. Are they causing additional stress for the abused spouse and her children? Yes. Are they and their disastrous approach to dealing with abuse often a main reason why abused spouses stay with their abusers? Yes.

Throughout this leaving process, you may find yourself facing deep disappointment and hurt because of the actions and comments from your local church leaders. If that's the case, I want to prepare you for how to handle it. So let's look at and refute biblical "reasons" they may take for their approach to abuse and what biblical support you actually do have for leaving.

MISGUIDED ADVICE

Here, in no particular order, are the most common misguided pieces of advice.

"It's Not Abuse"

One way to avoid dealing with abuse is simply to deny its existence. If you don't have abuse in the home, church leaders don't have to address it. When you describe in detail how you are being abused, your leaders don't believe you. They minimize the nature of the behavior and redefine it to mean something far less serious:

> "He just gets too intense when he's angry."
> "It could be far worse."
> "He feels misunderstood."
> "He's frustrated and annoyed."
> "His emotions get the better of him."

These leaders will do everything possible to stay away from you and your nasty situation. They will put off meeting with you, cancel appointments, not return calls or emails, and not follow through with promises they've made.

They want you to go away and leave them alone. They are uncomfortable with conflict and afraid of confronting your abuser.

If you were in the hospital with a fractured pelvis, they would call and visit and mobilize the church family to help you. Since you have only a fractured heart—and no good reason for it because they don't believe you're being abused—you're on your own.

> *Love like Christ's own love, which even meant dying on the cross, sets the standard for a husband's love—and actions—in caring for his wife.*

Their denial is a lie, and the Bible is clear about lying. Church leaders are to be shepherds of every one of their flock, protecting and caring for the sheep (see Acts 20:28; 1 Peter 5:2).

Church leaders are to address directly and without delay every spiritual issue in the church, no matter how difficult, painful, or awkward it might be (see 1 Cor. 5), and despite the negative, often unkind criticism they will receive for their actions.

"You Have to Submit, No Matter What"

Your leaders, using the submission passage in Ephesians 5:22–24, tell you that you must submit to your husband no matter how he's treating you. This is an incorrect and disgraceful interpretation of this passage. It takes the truth of a passage and ignores the rest of the Bible's teaching on the subject.

Part of the apostle Paul's instruction includes the nature of the husband's role: "The husband is the head of the wife, even *as Christ is the head of the church*" (v. 23, KJV, emphasis added). The husband is to treat his wife as Christ treats the church. Then, of course, nothing but love and care would characterize this "headship." It assures the wife's well-being.

Verse 25 instructs the husbands to "love your wives, just *as*

Christ also loved the church and gave Himself up for her" (emphasis added). Love like Christ's own love, which even meant dying on the cross, sets the standard for a husband's love—*and actions*—in caring for his wife.

And Paul goes on with the most practical words to husbands in Ephesians 5:28–29: "Husbands also ought to love their own wives *as their own bodies.* He who loves his own wife loves himself; for no one ever hated his own flesh, but *nourishes and cherishes it, just as Christ also does the church"* (emphasis added). Obviously, *the greater responsibility* is placed on the husband.

> *Submission does not apply in the extraordinary circumstance of a husband abusing his wife.*

Help for the marriage should begin with him. The apostle Paul is not recommending a wife submit to an abusive, sinning husband!

Submission does not apply in the extraordinary circumstance of a husband abusing his wife, and in fact would be contraindicated. Submission is not mentioned in any biblical passage that deals with confronting sin. That's because you do not submit to someone who is sinning.

What do you do with a sinner? You confront that person in the hope that he will turn from his sin. You do not submit to a sinner because doing so is enabling, accepting, and feeding that sinful behavior. Rather, you confront the sinner and his sin. Need some "proof"? See Matthew 18:15–17 and 5:23–24 below, and also 2 Samuel 12:1–7; 2 Corinthians 13:2; and Galatians 2:11.

> If your brother sins against you, go and tell him his fault, between you and him alone. If he listens to you, you

have gained your brother. But if he does not listen, take one or two others along with you, that every charge may be established by the evidence of two or three witnesses. If he refuses to listen to them, tell it to the church. And if he refuses to listen even to the church, let him be to you as a Gentile and a tax collector. (Matt. 18:15–17 ESV)

If you are presenting your offering at the altar, and there you remember that your brother has something against you, leave your offering there before the altar and go; first be reconciled to your brother, and then come and present your offering. (Matt. 5:23–24).

"It's Your Fault"

Your abuser will play the victim and blame you for causing his abusive behavior. In this surreal scenario, he admits he mistreats you, but all his mistreatment is your fault—as though saying so removes the sin. Incredibly, he will try to persuade your church leaders to believe this massive, evil lie.

Your leaders buy his ridiculous argument and tell you that:

You provoke his anger by failing in your "duties" or in many other ways.
You cause him to get frustrated.
You make him yell at you.
You make him hit you.
You make him shut down and ignore you.

They tell you that your tone of voice is the problem. Your criticism and lack of respect are the problem. Your withholding affection and sex is the problem. They say that if you hadn't done such and such, then he wouldn't have done what he did. It's as if "provoked" sin is excusable and need not be acknowledged and addressed. This is in direct opposition to biblical teaching (as referenced above).

So instead of confronting the real sinner, they confront you! You are causing your own mistreatment (they won't use the word *abuse*).

If your abuser is popular at church—in leadership, serving, helping others, a generous giver, charming, and friendly—it's even more likely your leaders will side with him and blame you.

On the other hand, even if he's quiet and not involved in church, they will often assume he's a good guy. These types of leaders have a built-in tendency to favor men over women. It's the old boys' club and, being a woman, you're not in it.

Everywhere sin is mentioned in the Bible, it's the complete fault and responsibility of the sinner. No one *makes* you sin. We're all tempted (see Matt. 6:13), but the Bible never says that anyone or anything is responsible except the one who chose to sin. A person sins because he wants to. He chooses to sin. The Bible condemns any attempt to blame God or anyone else for sin (see Rom. 1:18–32; James 1:13–16).

Your abuser's sin, his damaging behavior toward you, is 100 percent his fault. Not 70 percent, not 80 percent, not 90 percent. It's 100 percent his fault. That's what the Bible teaches.

"If You Keep Loving Him, He'll Change and Stop His Sinful Behavior"

This advice is one of the classics church leaders use. They tell you that if you continue to love and pursue your husband, he will respond eventually (they don't say how long it will take—a month, six months, a year, five years?). He will stop the abuse and love you back.

They support this approach by quoting the great love chapter of the Bible, 1 Corinthians 13 (I quoted this passage in chapter 5). They also often use 1 Peter 3:1–2: "Wives, be subject to your own husbands so that even if any of them are disobedient to the word, they may be won over without a word by the behavior of their wives, as they observe your pure and respectful behavior."

This approach—and these Scriptures—are directed to a decent, normal, and loving husband who is a believer. The Epistles of Peter (who was married) are written to believers (see 1 Peter 1:1–9, 2 Peter 1:1–2). *Even if any of them are disobedient to the word* may refer to many things, but in no way describes abuse. Such behavior would not be expected of a believing husband.

> *This* keep on loving him, and he'll change *approach also contradicts the Bible's teaching on husband-and-wife roles.*

If quoting this passage, then church leaders today should also include the context of these verses, such as 1 Peter 3:7: "Likewise, husbands, live with your wives in an understanding way, showing honor to the woman as the weaker vessel, since they are heirs with you of the grace of life, so that your prayers may not be hindered" (ESV). You currently don't have a decent, normal, and loving husband like that. You have an abuser, a man who continues to sin in a serious way.

Instead of having a 1 Peter 3:7 kind of husband, you have a 2 Timothy 3:2–7 husband. The list of awful, damaging behaviors in this passage begins with the phrase *lovers of self.* Your abuser will be untouched and unchanged by your love and pursuit of him. In fact, you will be enabling and supporting his sinful, abusive behavior.

If you continue to try to love him and meet his needs as a strategy to get him to see what he is doing to you and the marriage, he'll think everything is fine. He'll think he has no reason to change. He'll continue to damage you and your children. *It is vital for you to accept this.*

This *keep on loving him, and he'll change* approach also contradicts the Bible's teaching on husband-and-wife roles. Your leaders are telling you to lead the way in loving him. That's not your role. The Bible teaches that the husband is to be the leader in the marriage (see Eph. 5:22–24). And consider the qualifications of elders and deacons: "Deacons must be husbands of one wife, and good managers of their children and their own households" (1 Tim. 3:12; see also vv. 4–5).

And as I mentioned earlier, the husband is to love his wife *"as Christ also loved the church and gave Himself up for her"* (Eph. 5:25, emphasis added). Christ's love is the ultimate in caring, selfless, sacrificial love.

Most certainly the Bible tells the wife to love her husband (see Titus 2:4), but perhaps because of the difference between men and women, the primary command to love is given to *husbands* (see Eph. 5:25, 28; Col. 3:19). The husband is taught to take the initiative and love his wife on a much deeper level. The responsibility for the success or failure of the marriage is, biblically, laid squarely on the husband's shoulders.

"You Have to Stay with Him"

Your church leaders tell you the Bible teaches that unless your husband has committed adultery (see Matt. 5:32) or is an unbeliever who has abandoned you (see 1 Cor. 7:15), you cannot divorce your husband *or separate* from him.

They will equate separation with divorce, though Scripture

addresses only divorce. Many leaders believe that separation is the first step to divorce. That is simply not true. Of course, it often happens this way, but it's because at the point of separation, the couple had no plan that could lead to reconciliation, saving the marriage, and building a beautiful new one. In reality, separation will be the one step that could *save* the marriage, rather than lead to its end.

My plan recommends only separation, and separation is the first step to safety and protection for you and your children. Depending on your abuser's reaction, separation can also result in his repentance and change.

The Bible provides plenty of support for separation from a serious sinner. I believe a loving God allows separation from an abuser because He knows and grieves over the suffering and damage you and your kids are experiencing.

Your church leaders may tell you that God wants you to suffer. They say that suffering is part of His plan for you and your children. They quote verses such as Acts 5:41, which states that Christians are honored for suffering for the cause of Christ. Enduring abuse is not suffering for Christ! It does not glorify God. It does not advance the gospel of Jesus Christ. They may also present passages such as Romans 5:3–4 or 1 Peter 1:6–7 to justify your continuing to live in an unhealthy, even toxic, situation. Enduring abuse only destroys you and your children. It continues to destroy what love is left and the chance to save the marriage. God wants you to get away from it.

I've actually heard church leaders use the book of Hosea to urge abused wives to stay with their spouses. Seriously? Hosea's message is a prophecy concerning the covenant between God and Israel. God chose to send a powerful message about this covenant and His love and forgiveness by having Hosea stay with an adulterous and abusive wife.

This book of the Bible can in no way be interpreted to apply to anyone but Hosea and Gomer. Hosea does not teach a spouse to stay with an abusive partner! I tell abused wives: "If God appears to you and tells you to stay with your abuser, do it. If not, don't do it." The message of Hosea is one of God's everlasting love for His people and His forgiveness. If you are abused and leave your spouse, it does not mean that you do not love him or will not forgive him. Just the opposite.

Here are some Bible verses that lend support for leaving an abusive spouse:

- God presents a clear example of a wife escaping her abusive husband in 1 Samuel 25. (I devote an entire chapter to discussing this story.)
- "Leave the presence of a fool" (Prov. 14:7). Your abuser is a fool.
- Don't give honor to a fool (Prov. 26:8). In a way, you honor your abuser by staying with him, allowing him and others to believe he's a good husband.
- "Do not throw your pearls before pigs" (Matt. 7:6). Yes, your abuser is the pig in this analogy. In other words, get distance from a sinner and do not allow yourself to be vulnerable in front of him.
- Have no social contact with an unrepentant sinner (Matt. 18:17). This fits your abuser.
- Shun all who cause divisions (Rom. 16:17). Your abuser obviously is causing division in a sacred, God-ordained relationship.
- Have no contact with a person who continues in sexual sin (1 Cor. 5). Even if your abuser isn't into sexual sin, he's into serious sin, and I think this passage applies to him.

- If someone is living a sinful lifestyle, stay away from him (2 Thess. 3:6). Your abuser is living a sinful lifestyle.
- Avoid men who are guilty of this list of sins (2 Tim. 3:1–7). Your abuser is guilty of a number of these sins.

CHECK OUT YOUR PASTOR
AND YOUR CHRISTIAN THERAPIST

Find out how your pastor handles abuse. Call him, write him, or sit down with him, and ask him how he deals with an abusive spouse. Don't give details about your situation before being certain he has the correct, biblical approach to abuse.

If he subscribes to any of the damaging views we've covered in this chapter, tell him nothing about your situation and look for a church in which the pastor follows a godly, biblical approach to abuse.

Follow the same procedure when you are looking for a Christian therapist. Be wary of using anyone who does not hold at least a master's degree and a professional license. You also need a therapist with experience working with abuse.

Ask the therapists you contact how they deal with abuse. Even licensed professionals with experience can be clueless when it comes to abuse.

So be wary of church leaders, pastors, and therapists who use the Bible incorrectly when it comes to abusive husbands and will only cause you more harm.

CHAPTER 8

The Lies
That Make
You Stay

We've already mentioned several factors that can keep you from leaving your abuser:

- Your fears keep you with your abuser.
- Your concern that leaving is not biblical keeps you with your abuser.
- Your worry that your church leaders will not support your leaving keeps you with your abuser.

One more key factor keeps you chained to your abuser: you believe a pack of lies.

You hold your lies close because they help you cope with terrible, ongoing pain. A bunch of rationalizations, justifications, and excuses for staying are running through your head right now. In fact, your "reasons" for staying with your abuser are always in your head.

It's time for me to blow up your bogus reasons for staying with your abuser. This won't be pretty, so hang on.

YOUR LIES, MY TRUTH

In my work with abused spouses, all of them have believed and verbalized the same lies. Here are the most popular lies and my responses.

YOUR LIE: It isn't abuse.

MY TRUTH: Yes, it is. I'm a clinical psychologist in private practice for more than thirty years. I've graduated from two seminaries. Countless times, week after week, I have heard from the abused why they think they must not leave the ones who are hurting them. This lie allows the abuse to continue until their marriage may be beyond repair. I know what abuse is, and you are being abused.

If you receive vicious, personal attacks on a regular basis on what he thinks are your weaknesses as a wife, you are being abused. If you are forced to work and pay all the bills because he refuses to work, you are being abused. If you have to endure frequent temper outbursts with yelling, swearing, and property damage, you are being abused. If you keep finding pornography on your husband's devices and he refuses to stop this sin, you are being abused.

YOUR LIE: It's his wounds from the past—his childhood years—that make him act the way he does.

MY TRUTH: Plenty of persons have tough backgrounds and grow up to be loving spouses. He chooses not to work on his past issues. In my plan, he'll have a chance to heal from his wounds.

YOUR LIE: Maybe he has a chemical imbalance.

MY TRUTH: No, he's just mean. It's not chemical, it's character. There isn't a pill for that. If he has any chemical problems, he can address them with the appropriate physician(s). He will have an opportunity to do this.

YOUR LIE: He seems so sincere when he tells me my unhappiness is my fault.

MY TRUTH: Oh, he's sincere. Absolutely sincere. He is a consummate liar who believes his own lies. He'd pass a lie detector test. But his lies are still lies. You know what is true: instead of loving you, he is hurting you. That's truth. That's reality.

YOUR LIE: He does apologize on occasion.

MY TRUTH: So what? His apologies are meaningless if he continues the abusive behavior. They are even deceptive and harmful because they keep you confused and living with him.

YOUR LIE: But I need to forgive and reconcile with him, don't I?

MY TRUTH: Yes and no. Yes, you need to forgive him. The Bible is clear that we must forgive all those who sin against us (see Matt. 18:21–35; Col. 3:13). No, you do not have to reconcile with him and stay with him. Reconciliation is completely different from forgiveness. The Bible teaches us not to reconcile with an

unrepentant sinner (see Matt. 18:15–17; 1 Cor. 5:9–13).
If he ever repents and proves over time that he has
genuinely changed, then and only then will you consider
reconciliation.

YOUR LIE: Sometimes he's nice to me.
MY TRUTH: Really? Does this actually make your life okay?
His occasional niceness is like kicking the dog and then
tossing it a treat. And he's nice to you only to make
himself look good and to get what he wants, and keep
you there. You deserve niceness on a consistent, regular,
lifelong basis, motivated by love.

YOUR LIE: It's selfish of me to think of leaving him.
MY TRUTH: You're not being selfish! You have spent a long
time trying to meet his needs with the hope of changing
him. It's not selfish to protect yourself and your kids. It's a
God-given instinct. Plus, my plan is actually the best thing
for your abuser. It will give him a legitimate opportunity
to change. If you stay with him, you'll prevent the opportunity of saving the marriage.

YOUR LIE: He loves me!
MY TRUTH: No, he doesn't. He has no idea of what real
love is and what it means to show real love, and he has
no desire to learn. He loves only himself in a twisted and
sinful way.

YOUR LIE: He's a good man at heart.
MY TRUTH: He doesn't have a heart, and he's not a good
man. His behavior toward you and, indirectly, the children

is sinful and abusive. A good man with a heart does not act this way. Therefore, he is a sinful and abusive man.

YOUR LIE: We need marriage counseling.

MY TRUTH: No, you don't. *Not now.* The two of you need individual counseling; you, to stop tolerating his abuse, and him, to stop abusing you. In order for the counseling to be effective, you must *not* be living together. In that toxic situation, success can't happen. If—and it's a big if—he ever truly repents, that is, *changes*, then that will be the time for marriage counseling.

YOUR LIE: I can't tell others about the abuse because he will be humiliated, angry, and will get even more abusive. It will ruin his reputation.

MY TRUTH: His reputation is a lie that you have protected. The Bible, in Matthew 18 and other places, clearly teaches that you should expose his sin. He will be humiliated and angry. That's good, because it may motivate him to change. Keep in mind, you will be *away from him and safe* when you expose his sin.

YOUR LIE: I don't want others to know because I will be humiliated.

MY TRUTH: You are already humiliating yourself by tolerating his abuse as though you deserved it, which you do not. It will be hard when others know the truth. But you know what is worse than that? Staying with your abuser. When others learn the truth because of your bravery, they can provide the real support you need.

YOUR LIE: He'll change in time.

MY TRUTH: No, he won't. Time doesn't change an abuser.
You are wasting precious time by staying with him.
Unless God performs a miracle in his life, you and you
alone are the key to change for you all.

YOUR LIE: I still love him.

MY TRUTH: I know you hate with all your being to say you
don't love him. But stop it! Just
stop it. Why would you love
someone who treats you so badly?
Why would you love someone
who harms your precious children
with his abuse of you? You don't
love him. You love the idea of who
he can be as a husband. You love a
fantasy. Once you get past denial,
you won't love him. Not what he
is now. You will be disgusted with
him. What you have is addiction,
not love. You're used to being
abused. Tolerating abuse is an entrenched pattern for you.
It's what you do. You're good at it. You have an addiction,
and it's accepting his abuse. That's different from love.

> When you're more emotionally healthy, you will feel righteous anger, and that anger will fuel your escape.

Separating from him will give you a chance to understand what love really means, from people who support
you and don't hurt you.

YOUR LIE: I will never divorce him.

MY TRUTH: So it's more important to stay married than save
yourself and your kids from being destroyed? I tell you

emphatically: I never recommend divorce or even discuss it. That's because I believe in the power of God (see Matt. 19:26; Phil. 4:13), in the sanctity of His institution of marriage, and in the faith of individuals who trust Him. A decision like that must be God's, and He will direct you. My plan actually gives you the best chance—the only chance—for a changed husband and a happy marriage.

YOUR LIE: To follow your plan, I'd have to be angry—really angry. And I'm not an angry person.

MY TRUTH: In this monumentally significant situation, you should be an angry person. Anger at sin is righteous (see Eph. 4:26). Jesus was angry at sin (see Matt. 21:12–13). Abigail got angry (see 1 Sam. 25). When you're more emotionally healthy, you will feel righteous anger, and that anger will fuel your escape. I know you're not angry—yet. You *are* sad, depressed, and defeated. With God's help, we're going to change that.

YOUR LIE: I'll never be strong enough to leave him.

MY TRUTH: Not now. But you can get strong enough to leave him by following my steps. And when you say and believe that you'll never be strong enough to leave him, you are limiting what God can do in your life! You are saying God can't get you out. God can do anything, and He can empower you to get out. But you have to want the help.

YOUR LIE: Dr. Clarke, you seem so harsh and brutal. You are not very compassionate.

MY TRUTH: I am compassionate, because I am on a rescue mission. I believe it's God's rescue mission. God wants to release you from your prison of abuse, and He can use my plan to do it. Your life is bereft of compassion and is harsh and brutal. I'm harsh and brutal to get your attention and motivate you to get away from your abuser and begin a new life. Being nice, sweet, and passive when we are talking about sin and sadness won't get you out of this destructive relationship.

I hope and pray I have helped you recognize whether or not your man is acting in abusive ways. It's a hard and painful truth, but the sooner you stop believing the lies in your head and accept the facts, the sooner you can start the process of getting away from your abuser.

It's time to move you past what's left of your denial and get you ready for war.

PART 3

Why You Can Get Out

CHAPTER 9

Get Out of Denial and Get Ready for War

It was my first session with a couple, both in their mid-forties and married for twenty years. He sat on my couch looking smug, confident, and at ease. He should have looked embarrassed, insecure, and agitated. But he had no reason to worry. He knew that, no matter what he did, his wife would never leave him.

He had a nasty temper and blew up in a rage several times a week. He swore, yelled, and occasionally pushed her to the ground. She had never called the police.

He was also a serial adulterer. When I asked how many women he'd had sex with, he couldn't give me a number. It was so high, he couldn't remember. He'd had two long-term adulterous relationships, one for a year and one for two years.

She knew about all these adulteries, but continued to live with him. She didn't even seem that upset about his outrageous sexual sin. She'd gotten used to it. She kept dragging him to marriage seminars, pastors, and therapy offices like mine.

Here's the best part of the story. (I say that facetiously. Actually, it's the worst part.) He admitted he was still seeing the woman in the second long-term adulterous relationship. After two years, they were still going strong. And . . . wait for it . . . his wife admitted she was well aware of the ongoing adultery.

"What are you doing here?" I asked Mr. Smug.

"My wife asked me to come," he said.

I turned to the wife. "Here's the more important question. What are *you* doing here?"

"Well, I want a better marriage," she said.

"You don't have a marriage," I told her. "You have a man who is sleeping with someone else. He knows you know what he's doing and that you'll do nothing about it. There is no marriage work to be done at this time."

I told the husband that he needed to stop the adultery immediately and get into individual therapy for his sex addiction, anger, and abusive behavior. He smiled at me. He was never going to do that.

I told his wife she needed individual therapy to heal from the wounds he'd inflicted on her and to figure out why she continued to tolerate his abuse. I added: "I'd give him two minutes to end this current adulterous relationship and agree to get individual therapy. If he refuses, kick him out. If he won't leave, I will work with you to get you ready to leave."

The wife was furious with me. "You haven't helped us at all!" she spat out. "What a waste of time!"

"First of all," I replied, "there is no *us*. It's just him and the woman he's having an affair with. Second, I gave you a clear plan. You might not like it, but it's the best plan for you."

She got up, gave me a dagger look, and stomped out of my office, slamming the back door of my office building on her way out. She had joined a long parade of codependents who were not ready to stop living with an abusive spouse.

This wife was used to his abuse. She was comfortable with it. It was a familiar continuation of the abuse she'd suffered growing up. She was not going to do anything about it.

You are this woman. Your husband may not be a serial adulterer and "rageaholic," but he's a serial something else, and it's abusive. And you continue to tolerate his abuse. It's a pattern. It's been going on for years. He's not going to stop it. It's your responsibility to get away from him and his abusive behavior.

I'm telling you—and I believe God is telling you—that you don't have to stay with your abusive spouse. Unless you want to, like this miserable wife.

Don't slam the door on me.

I admit it. I'm being tough on you. I will not entertain or consider even one of your excuses for staying with your abuser. I am hammering away at your massive wall of denial. It's your denial and the lies you believe connected to it that keep you with your abuser.

I want to get you out of denial and into cold, clearheaded reality. I want to save you and your kids. *God* wants to save you and your kids!

God has a great plan for your life, and it does not include staying in an abusive relationship. Enduring abuse is Satan's plan for your life.

I want you to get out of denial, get rid of your codependency, and get ready to leave. Right now, you are his captive. His prisoner. Locked in a cell. Tortured emotionally on a regular basis. I'm going to show you exactly how to wage a secret war against your jailer and get away from him.

GOD DOESN'T WANT YOU TO BE ABUSED

I want you to really stop and hear this. Intellectually, you know what I'm about to tell you. This time, I want these biblical truths to connect with your heart.

You are precious to God. Of the hundreds of references to His love for you, here are two: Psalm 31:7 and Ephesians 2:4. He made you. You are unique. He's crazy about *you*. You are priceless to Him. He feels the same way about your children.

> *Do you think for a second that God wants you, His child, to be abused? To be broken? Never!*

God formed you in your mother's womb (see Ps. 139:13). God sent His only Son, Jesus, to die for you and for the forgiveness of your sins, so that you could have a personal relationship with Him (see John 3:16).

Do you think for a second that God wants you, His child, to be abused? To be broken? To be destroyed by your abuser? To live in ongoing misery, fear, disappointment, and hopelessness?

Never!

In Matthew 18, Jesus gives a severe warning to anyone who causes a child harm, especially harm to his or her spiritual life: "Whoever causes one of these little ones who believe in Me to sin, it is better for him that a heavy millstone be hung around his neck, and that he be drowned in the depths of the sea" (v. 6).

You are one of those little ones! And so is each of your children.

IF YOU STAY, IT'S ON YOU

I recently saw a lady I had counseled along with her abusive husband twenty years earlier. Twenty years prior she was still young and healthy and had young kids at home. At that time, I told her I couldn't do a thing for her marriage.

Her husband was a big man at church, and everyone there loved him. At home, he was verbally abusive and into pornography. He came to therapy only to check the box and look good. He refused my recommendation to get individual therapy for his abusive behavior and porn addiction.

He didn't like me because I called him out and wouldn't waste time in couple counseling. I didn't like him either.

I met with this lady privately and told her I would work with her in individual therapy. I told her she needed to get strong enough to leave her abusive husband. I told her I could help her figure out why she tolerated his abuse. I told her that she could, with the right approach and God's power, live a life free from his abuse.

I told her if she stayed with her husband, she'd lose her physical health. She'd lose her emotional health. She'd lose her kids. She'd lose her chance to live a life of peace and fulfillment.

She said she wasn't sure what to do. She told me she'd get back to me. She never did.

When she walked into my office again, twenty years later, I didn't recognize her. She wasn't old, but she looked old and worn out. She came with her adult daughter because she was too depressed and anxious to drive.

She had obviously decided to stay with her husband. She said they had seen a few therapists in marriage counseling, but nothing had changed. He had continued the abuse and, finally, had left her a year ago.

Physically, she was a wreck: she had heart and back issues. Emotionally, she was a wreck: she was chronically depressed and anxious. Her adult children hadn't turned on her, but it was almost worse than that: they pitied her, felt sorry for her, and had no respect for her.

Her daughter told me that she and the other kids loved their mom, but were tired of hearing her complaints about their dad. They didn't believe all the stuff about the abuse, and they didn't care anyway. That was all in the past. They wanted her to move on with her life.

It was too late for this lady. She missed her opportunity to get out. She was broken and alone.

I urge you, don't end up like this woman. Don't stay with your abuser and give up everyone and everything that is dear to you.

I can't make you prepare to leave this horrible situation. And I can't make you leave. You can choose to stay in denial and stay with your abuser. Staying in this situation is what most do. And in 99.9 percent of the cases, their unhappiness and wounding continue. Inevitably, separation and divorce result anyway.

Many of my abused clients have chosen to stay. But know this: if you decide to stay, all of the resulting consequences will be your responsibility.

All the damage, problems, and misery you and your kids will continue to experience will be partly your responsibility now. Don't play the martyr. Don't complain.

HOW THE ABUSIVE GAME IS PLAYED

I was sitting with an abuser and his wife. Ten minutes into the first session, I already knew he was an abuser. After thirty years of working with abusive men, I can spot them quickly.

The wife was telling me a long list of her attempts to change him and their marriage: "I took him to our pastor, but he didn't go back after just two meetings. I took him to four marriage counselors, but he lasted only a few sessions with each. I took him to three marriage seminars, but he slept through two and left one early. I asked him to read probably ten marriage books, but he never did. I had some friends do an intervention, but it made no difference."

"Aren't you getting tired of the game?" I asked her.

"What game?" she said.

"The game of you try and he resists," I replied. "As long as he knows that you still care and still make attempts to change him, he has no motivation to change. You're not going anywhere. You'll never leave him. It's a great game for him. He actually enjoys it."

"So what should I do?" she asked.

I asked her husband to leave my office. Then I answered: "Stop all efforts to change him and the marriage. I'll work with you to change you, to get you strong enough to leave him."

"No, I'm not ready to stop trying," she said. "I've signed us up for a marriage intensive next month."

I told her I couldn't help her, and that was that.

I wonder if I'll see her in twenty years.

Stop trying to change him. Stop trying to improve your marriage. Stop trying to love him so he'll love you back. Stop reading marriage books. Stop listening to marriage podcasts. Stop googling, "How do I save my marriage?" Stop asking him to attend marriage seminars.

All these efforts are a waste of time. And they have never worked. They never will work in your situation. These approaches are like taking booster shots and vitamins. But you have a life-threatening disease!

You try; he resists and continues to treat you in abusive ways. Enough is enough!

YOUR SECRET CAMPAIGN AND WAR

You will wage a secret campaign to leave your abuser. You are planning to leave not a loving, protective, supportive husband but someone draining your life of its joy. Only a few, key supporters will know what you're doing.

Your abuser will know nothing. If he knew, he'd do whatever he could to stop you. He would become even more abusive in order to crush your escape plan and get you back in line. If word is out about your plan, he will discredit your behavior and make sure everyone knows you are the one who is doing wrong. Therefore, the man who has always had to know everything you are doing will know *absolutely nothing* about your campaign to leave him.

When you've gone through my steps and are ready, you will take the kids and leave him without any warning. From a position of safety and security and distance, you will offer him—through your trusted supporters—an opportunity to repent and win you back. How he can win you back you will spell out in detail for his consideration and guidance.

You will never live with him again unless he is completely repentant, is a completely new and godly man, and has helped you heal from the damage he's done to you and the kids.

Getting ready to leave, leaving, dealing with his response to your leaving, and his response to your requirements for him to win you back and heal the marriage will be a very difficult, demanding journey. In fact, you are going to war against your abuser. It's a war you can win, but it's still a war. As frightening as the prospect is, it is either leaving or allowing the inevitable, irreversible damage to go on.

As you move into this war and fight, I want you to carry with you these two Bible passages:

(1) "We are afflicted in every way, but not crushed; perplexed, but not despairing; persecuted, but not abandoned; struck down, but not destroyed" (2 Cor. 4:8–9). You are afflicted by your abuser, but you're still standing. You are perplexed by your abuser, but not hopeless. You're certainly persecuted by your abuser, but not forsaken by God. You are struck down by your abuser, but you are still alive and kicking. Your abuser cannot destroy you unless you stay and allow it. You can choose to take action, follow my campaign, remove yourself from the abuse, and live a new life of freedom and happiness.

God will personally go with you on your journey of escape.

(2) "Be strong and courageous, do not be afraid or in dread of them, for the LORD your God is the One who is going with you. He will not desert you or abandon you" (Deut. 31:6). God will personally go with you on your journey of escape. He will not leave your side. He can get you out.

THIS COULD BE YOU

She was in her mid-thirties with three small children. She had a decent job. She loved Jesus and attended church faithfully. She loved her husband. Unfortunately, he didn't love her. He only loved himself.

From very early in the marriage, he had been verbally abusing her. She was never good enough for him. She wasn't pretty enough. She wasn't thin enough. She didn't make enough money. She wasn't a good enough cook. She didn't give him enough sex. She wasn't responsive enough in bed.

Lately, he had started attacking her ability as a mother. She couldn't discipline them the right way. She didn't dress them the right way. She couldn't do their hair the right way.

The final straw, the reason she was in my office, had occurred a few days earlier in the hospital. A family member she was close to had just died. Devastated, she was sobbing outside the relative's room.

Her husband walked over to her. She thought he was going to comfort and console her. Fat chance. He chose that moment of intense grief to inform her that he was very unhappy in their marriage. He let her know she had better improve as a wife or he would divorce her.

"Have you finally had enough?" I asked her.

"Yes, I think so," she replied, "I don't want to keep living with a man who treats me so badly."

"Good, let's get to work."

It took six months for her to be ready to leave her abuser.

When he came home one evening to find her and the kids gone, he was beyond furious. He immediately went to a lawyer and filed for divorce.

She was sad that he made this sinful decision, but she realized it was his choice. She offered him a clear path to win her back, and he stuck with his decision to divorce her. She got through the divorce process and is happy and at peace. Money is tight, but she's making it. The abuser still causes problems, but he's not in control of her life anymore. He's an annoyance, nothing more.

She is now engaged to a fine, godly man who genuinely loves her and her children. His ex-wife abused him for years, so he understands what she went through.

You can be this woman. Her escape to freedom can be your story.

It's going to be hard to make the decision to leave, to take the steps to prepare, and then to actually follow through and leave. Incredibly hard. It will be the most difficult thing you have ever done. But it's the right thing to do. God, your heavenly Father, doesn't want you to be abused.

CHAPTER 10

God Says, "I Want You to Get Out"

In His wisdom and mercy and marvelous grace, God wants you to know—without a shadow of a doubt—that it is okay to leave your abuser. In chapter 7, you read the verses that provide biblical support for leaving.

But God doesn't stop there. He goes much further than teaching it is permissible to leave your abuser. God makes it clear that He *wants* you to leave your abuser.

That's a bold assertion, isn't it?

I believe, with complete and total confidence, that God will support you in your decision to leave your abusive partner. I do not make that statement lightly. It's of the utmost importance to me, and

> *I believe, with complete and total confidence, that God will support you in your decision to leave your abusive partner.*

I'm sure to you as well, that I back up my position biblically.

So how can I make that seemingly outrageous claim that God wants you to leave? Because of the story of Abigail and Nabal.

ABIGAIL AND HER ABUSER

We find exhibit A in the Bible's case for getting away from your abuser in 1 Samuel 25. This issue is so critical to God that He includes in His Word a detailed account of one abused wife's exit strategy.

Abigail was living a nightmare! Why? The answer is one word: *Nabal*. One of the true dirtbags of the Bible, Nabal is a classic example of an abusive husband. This is how the Bible describes him: "The man was harsh and evil in his dealings" (1 Sam. 25:3). *Evil* is a pretty strong word.

In verse 25, Abigail uses some choice words of her own to describe Nabal. Referring to him as "this worthless man," she says that "stupidity is with him." When your own wife calls you a worthless fool, you must be a dirtbag.

As a clinical psychologist (that's me) reading 1 Samuel 25, I see more nasty personality traits that emerge. He was incredibly selfish. He was ungrateful. He was mean. He was bitingly sarcastic. He was arrogant. He had no empathy. Based on what you've read so far, you know how I would diagnose him: a narcissist. He didn't care about anyone but himself. It was all about him.

As a person, Abigail was a completely different story. Even though compared to Nabal any woman would seem like a saint, Abigail was very impressive. The Bible describes her as "intelligent and beautiful" (1 Sam. 25:3). Other wonderful, admirable traits emerge from a reading of her story. Abigail had tremendous empathy. She was decisive and efficient, a natural leader. She was courageous, humble, and insightful. She was a good, solid woman. Nabal did not deserve Abigail. Obviously.

And there's something else. She was stuck in a horrific marriage to a world-class abuser, with no way out.

In that day, a wife had no rights. She was her husband's property. A wife had two choices if she was unhappy with her husband: she could endure how he treated her and stay married to him, or she could endure how he treated her and stay married to him. If a wife didn't sit down and shut up, her husband could do very bad things to her. Check out many places in the world today, and you'll see that not much has changed.

Abigail was in a hopeless situation, right? Wrong! God did what God does when He wants a wife to get out of an abusive marriage. And He always wants a wife to get out of an abusive marriage. God intervened and presented Abigail with an opportunity to escape her painful, destructive marriage. Abigail stood up, spoke up, and changed the direction of her life.

Here is Abigail's story. Prepare to have your mind blown.

FROM NIGHTMARE TO NEW LIFE

Nabal was a very wealthy narcissist. "He had three thousand sheep and a thousand goats" (1 Sam. 25:2). In today's world, that's like having a Palm Beach mansion, a place on Martha's Vineyard, and millions in the bank.

David, Israel's king-in-waiting, sent some of his men to ask Nabal for provisions to sustain him and his men. As part of the request for help, David had his emissaries mention the fact that he had protected Nabal's workers during the recent shearing season. Being filthy rich, Nabal easily could have given David what he needed.

Instead, Nabal refused to give David anything. True to his nasty nature, Nabal said no in a contemptuous, sarcastic, and insulting fashion. David was furious and immediately planned to storm Nabal's camp with four hundred armed men. He was going to slaughter Nabal, slaughter every male in his household, and take by force the food he needed.

When Abigail learned of David's plan, she flew into action. With the help of some male servants, she gathered a large amount of food and set out to intercept David and his men. Her courage was remarkable in two significant ways. One, she gathered the food without telling her husband. That broke all the rules of marriage of that day. Wives didn't just take that kind of dramatic, independent action. Nabal could have punished her severely for acting alone. Two, she boldly traveled to confront a deadly, rage-filled warrior and his four hundred bloodthirsty soldiers. Talk about a risk! She literally put her life on the line. Yet thanks to her quick thinking and bravery, Abigail saved Nabal and her household from a massacre.

David was impressed with Abigail and blessed her for saving him from a rash course of action.

When Abigail assertively told Nabal what had happened and how close he had come to utter disaster, he suffered from what was apparently a heart attack or a stroke. He died about ten days later. The truth is, God took him out: "The LORD struck Nabal and he died" (v. 38). Nabal's funeral likely was not well attended. And probably it was a time of rejoicing rather than mourning.

When David heard of Nabal's death, he thanked God for getting rid of this evil man. And he wasted no time asking Abigail to marry him. Abigail was thrilled to accept. It was certainly a strange courtship but a beautiful ending to the story.

IF ABIGAIL CAN DO IT, SO CAN YOU

If you're married to an abusive husband, or if you are dating or living with an abusive man, the account of Abigail's escape from Nabal is God's way of sending a message. It's a message of hope, motivation, and practical instruction. Here are the facts:

- Abigail was married to a mean, abusive man.
- When Abigail's family was threatened as a result of her husband's actions, she took action.
- Abigail acted to protect her family, including herself, not to protect her sinning husband.
- Abigail told others the truth about her husband.
- Abigail enlisted the help of others in her escape plan.
- Abigail did not tell her husband what she was doing.
- At the right time, Abigail confronted her husband with the truth.
- Her husband did not change.
- Abigail chose to change.
- When God offered Abigail a way out of the abuse, she took it at risk to herself.
- God approved of Abigail's assertive behavior and blessed her for it.
- Abigail got away from her husband and enjoyed a new life of freedom and adventure.

Go back and read the above section again. But this time insert your name in place of Abigail's name. Walk in Abigail's shoes (sandals). You're already walking in her shoes, aren't you? I know you can relate to her. You are suffering every day in a relationship very much like Abigail's.

Follow Abigail's gutsy example and stop tolerating your man's abusive treatment. You are Abigail. Get out!

SEIZE YOUR OPPORTUNITY

God provided Abigail an opportunity to get out of an abusive relationship, and she seized it. Through Abigail's story, God is providing you with an opportunity to get out of your abusive relationship. This is your opportunity. Take it. Right here. Right now.

You may be thinking, *But, Dave, why can't God just kill my husband like He did for Abigail? That would be a lot easier than leaving him.* I don't blame you for thinking this. Many of my abused clients have thought it.

Through Abigail's story, God is providing you with an opportunity to get out of your abusive relationship. This is your opportunity. Take it.

Though God could certainly kill your husband, He's probably not going to do that. What He will do is give you His presence and power so that you can leave him.

You're feeling anxious, aren't you? You're thinking, *I'm not ready. I'm not strong enough. I don't know what to do. It's such a huge, life-changing step.*

I know you are not strong enough now to take action. I know your fears, and I know they are very real. I get that. Though the Bible does not mention it, I believe God spent time preparing Abigail for her aggressive action against Nabal.

And He's preparing you for your exit as well. That's why God has you reading this book.

Now is the time. You're ready to begin the process of leaving your abuser.

PART 4

How
to
Get Out

CHAPTER 11

Get Spiritually Healthy

I'm a bottom-line guy, so here's the bottom line: you need God in order to get out of your abusive relationship. Just like Abigail, you must rely on God as you take my action steps.

My escape plan works. But it's tough. *Very* tough. There is no way you can do it on your own. You and God can pull it off. God can do anything. As Matthew 19:26 says, "With God all things are possible."

To escape successfully, you need God's power and strength. You need His provision of perseverance, His wisdom, His patience, His guidance, and His grace. You need God's mercy as well as His righteous anger. And you need His love and His peace.

> *To make sure you have God with you in this upcoming war, you need to have a relationship with Him and stay close to Him.*

To make sure you have God with you in this upcoming war, you need to have a relationship with Him and stay close to Him. When you know Him, and are working to stay close to Him, here is what God will do for you:

> When you pass through the waters, I will be with you;
> And through the rivers, they will not overflow you.
> When you walk through the fire, you will not be scorched,
> Nor will the flame burn you. (Isa. 43:2)

To have access to all God offers (and the above list is only a part of what He offers), you must have a personal relationship with God through His Son, Jesus Christ. This is what makes you a Christian.

I'll make this simple, because the Bible's message about how you become a Christian is simple. There is one God, and that is the God of the Bible. There is only one way to establish a relationship with God, and that is through His Son, Jesus Christ. Christianity *is* Christ.

Here is Jesus Christ, in His own words: "I am the way, and the truth, and the life; no one comes to the Father except through Me" (John 14:6).

A Christian is someone who has a *personal* relationship with God through Christ. God sent Jesus to die for your sins—all the things you've done wrong—so you can have a relationship with God: "For God so loved the world, that He gave His only Son, so that everyone who believes in Him will not perish, but have eternal life" (John 3:16).

The following passage describes what you must believe to become a Christian: "I handed down to you as of first importance what I also received, that Christ died for our sins according to the Scriptures, and that He was buried, and that He was raised on the third day according to the Scriptures" (1 Cor. 15:3–4).

When you believe the following three truths, you become a

Christian and you have a personal relationship with God through His Son:

- Jesus died for your sins
- Jesus was buried
- Jesus rose from the dead

If you have never made this decision, I urge you to believe in Jesus as your Savior. You can begin your relationship with God through Jesus right now by saying and believing the words in this brief prayer:

> Dear God,
> I know I'm a sinner. I've made many mistakes and have sinned in my life. I realize my sin separates me from You, a holy God. I believe that Your Son, Jesus Christ, died for my sins, was buried, and rose from the dead. I believe that You have forgiven me of all my sins. I give my life to You now.

If you prayed this prayer and actually believe the truths you prayed, you now know God, and He will walk with you—and carry you at times—on your journey of escape. You can give Him all of your worries and tell Him what you're afraid of. Just as you would cast the line of a fishing pole into a lake, you can "cast all your anxiety on Him, because He cares about you" (1 Peter 5:7).

GROW CLOSER TO JESUS

Four behaviors are critical to growing closer and closer to Jesus. As you work on these behaviors, you will develop the power and confidence to follow my "Escape from Abuse" plan.

Spend Time Alone with Jesus

The first behavior is to have a daily quiet time with Jesus. During this time, it's just Jesus and you, spending ten to fifteen minutes together in a private, quiet place. Use part of this time to pray, which means talking to Jesus. You can worship Him, confess your sins, ask for His infusion of power to help you eliminate sins from your life and resist temptation, thank Him for all He's doing for you, share your triumphs and troubles, and make requests. Also, read a few verses from the Bible in a version that clearly speaks to you, and spend a few minutes meditating and thinking about how you can apply the Bible's truths in your life.

Pray throughout the Day

The second behavior is to pray throughout your day. Jesus is with you everywhere you go, so keep talking to Him. Tell Him what's happening, what you're thinking and feeling when worry and anxiety creep in, and how you can see Him guiding you. Ask for His help, His wisdom, and His strength as you navigate the ups and downs of your day (see Phil. 4:6–7; James 1:5).

Regularly Attend Church

The third behavior is to attend a local church every week. The Bible teaches that we are to be part of a local church and not neglect attending (see Heb. 10:25). But don't just attend. Get involved! Join a small group, such as a Sunday adult Bible fellowship class, a regular weekly Bible study, a home-based group, or a Celebrate Recovery group. And find a place in your church to serve others.

Connect with a Spiritual Coach

The fourth behavior is to sign up with a spiritual coach. A spiritual coach can help you grow closer to Jesus. In fact, this person can make the difference between growth and growing careless and losing your closeness to Christ. Your spiritual coach should be a person of your own sex. That person can be a close Christian friend, an older mentor, or someone younger who has walked with Jesus for a few years. If you can't think of anyone, or if those you ask say no, ask your pastor to find you a coach.

Once you have identified the individual, here's how you ask this person to be your coach: "I want my relationship with Jesus to get better and deeper. I'm asking you to help me do that. Please meet with me once a week. We can do this by phone on the weeks we can't meet."

In these meetings, have your mentor ask you about the following:

How are you doing in your relationship with Jesus?
What actions have you taken to improve this relationship?
What insights have you gained from your Bible reading?
What have your spiritual struggles and victories been this week?
What are you praying about in your quiet times with Jesus?
How did last week's church service impact you?

Ultimately, your coach will hold you accountable, support and encourage you, pray with you, and stand with you in tough times.

Your spiritual coach will also be by your side as you work toward getting away from your abuser by providing support, accountability, and practical help.

WORKING IT OUT WITH GOD

The abused wife looked at me with sad eyes. "Why would God allow me to marry such an awful man?"

She asked a good question, and we spent the next few therapy sessions talking about it.

She was a Christian. She attended church regularly. But the abuse she was suffering had taken a fierce toll on her relationship with God. She worked through her resentments against Him. She was able to see the truth: None of what was happening was God's fault; it was her abuser's fault. He was the one responsible for all the pain she was experiencing.

In one session, she achieved some key insights: "I think it's easier to blame God than my abuser, because if I blame my abuser, I have to face the abuse and do something about it. If I choose to stay with my abuser, then it will be my fault that I'm experiencing this kind of treatment."

She asked God for forgiveness for blaming Him, and grew very close to Him during her preparations to leave her abuser. Her daily quiet times with Jesus were sweet and intimate. Her prayer life deepened. She joined a women's Bible study at her church.

God, her spiritual coach, and the women in her Bible study supported her as she took the necessary steps in my plan to get away from her abuser. Her closeness to God gave her the strength she needed to gain her freedom.

Once you have God on your side, as well as a spiritual coach, you, too, can grow stronger through your relationship with Jesus.

CHAPTER 12

Get a Team of Warriors

I met with a husband and wife who had been married fifteen years and had two kids in middle school. The wife had borderline personality disorder, and had been emotionally abusing her husband for the entire marriage.

I referred the wife to a female therapist for her personal issues. Not surprisingly, she never followed up. In her mixed-up, abusive mind, she was perfect and her husband was the problem.

As this husband and I worked on his emotional health and the escape plan, he gathered his team of warriors. His pastor, who knew his wife well and was supportive, readily agreed to join his team.

Like many men, he didn't have any close male friends, so finding an accountability partner took a few months. His pastor gave him a list of candidates, and the first three didn't pan out. One didn't have time, one didn't want to get involved in his marital issues, and one would not go beyond a superficial relationship.

Number four was a winner. He was a godly older man whose ex-wife had abused him for years. He understood my client's pain.

He was there for my client up to the day he left his wife and beyond.

The younger abused husband had a chaotic, dysfunctional family, so he signed up only one younger sister for his team. He added two other men he met at a men's Bible study. These four men, and the other men in that small group, gave him much-needed emotional and spiritual support during his escape process.

> *No one has ever escaped an abusive relationship alone. No one.*

I referred him to a tough, experienced female attorney in my local area. You wouldn't want to meet this woman in a dark alley or in a courtroom. She protected his financial interests and his time with his children.

As for the tough, experienced Christian therapist, he had me. I helped him heal from the wounds of his family of origin and the wounds of his abusive wife. I kept him on a path of escape and helped him and his kids leave.

No one has ever escaped an abusive relationship alone. No one. Abigail didn't get out by acting on her own. She had help by enlisting others. You also need help to conquer your fears and your feelings of false guilt and take action.

Don't waste your time trying to escape the abuse alone. You'll never make it.

The Bible says, "By wise guidance you will wage war, and in an abundance of counselors there is victory" (Prov. 24:6).

The phrase *one another* is found fifty-eight times in the New Testament. Fifty-eight times! God makes it clear that we need people. The church itself—meaning not a building or an organization, but people—was founded by Christ so Christians can help one another. The Bible is filled with verses instructing us to support, love, encourage, confront, and be accountable to one another.

You, like everyone else, need support.

THE PEOPLE YOU NEED—AND DON'T NEED

You'll need a support team as you make your plans to leave your abuser. Every member on your team must be a strong, unwavering supporter of your decision to no longer tolerate the abuse in your marriage and fight back against your sinning husband. Every team member must be on board with your plan.

You don't need a team member who tries to see things from your abusive husband's point of view. You don't need a team member who wants you and your husband to get marriage counseling. This isn't a marriage counseling case. At least not yet. It's the case of an abused wife taking a stand—now—and saying, "Enough is enough," and forcing her husband to make a choice: "Change, or lose me."

You don't need a team member who recommends the *keep on loving him, and he'll eventually stop abusing you* approach. We are dealing with *abuse*, not a bad marriage. This thinking is not biblical. It doesn't work. It's like telling someone to keep on charming a poisonous cobra as it repeatedly bites her. You know what you ought to do: get away from the cobra!

Avoid all the passive, hand-wringing, wimpy, gutless enablers. They are everywhere, and their advice will lead only to a continued abusive relationship. Even if they mean well, these people don't get it and probably never will. And they have not been in your circumstances.

Every team member will agree to say nothing about your escape plan to your abuser. In fact, every member will agree to say nothing about you in every area to your abuser. When—not if—your abuser questions members of your team and wants information, they will simply reply with one statement only: "This is a matter between you and (*your name*)." Nothing more. End of conversation. Not to be brought up again.

Your abuser isn't stupid, and he'll know your team members are holding back information. Whatever. Your team members need to expect his pressure and hold the line by giving up zero information about you. They must be firm. I repeat: They must make one statement only; it's a subject that's between the two of you. No further discussion.

You need a team of fellow warriors in your campaign against your abuser. Though it may take a while to enlist everyone, it will be worth the effort.

Here's your team.

Your Pastor

Sit down with your pastor—or an associate pastor, if you attend a large church—and tell him everything about your abusive marriage. Ask him for his full support as you follow my escape plan. If you talk to an associate pastor, ask him to talk to the senior pastor and find out if he will support you as you plan to escape. You are not asking for advice and counsel other than what relates to your plan to leave your abuser. You have made that decision.

You will need the full, unqualified support of your senior pastor. You will need his spiritual support, which will include prayer and encouragement. You need his practical support, which may include financial gifts and a temporary place to live.

After you have left the home, you will need his agreement to be willing to confront your sinning husband. Give him this book to read.

His response to your request to confront your husband will tell you immediately what you need to know about him and his church leaders. Any of these responses from him will show you he will not support you:

- He refuses to confront your husband or have any church leaders confront him.
- He tells you he will not get involved in your marital issues.
- He says he will pray for you, but that's it. Nothing more.
- He blames you or implies you are to blame for your husband's sinful behavior.
- He tells you to stay in your home, overlook the abuse, and keep on loving your husband.
- He defers and refers you to a Christian counselor, washing his hands of the whole situation. You did not ask him for counseling. You asked him only to stand with you and to be willing to confront the abuser.

If your senior pastor will not support your escape, it's obvious he will not be on your team.

Tell him and the other church leaders nothing else about your situation. You may stay at the church for now for the sake of your kids and because you have solid, supportive friends there.

In the meantime, actively look for a local church whose senior pastor will support your departure from your abusive spouse. When you find this pastor, build your relationship with him and some key leaders in the church. You will be moving to this new church when you leave your home.

Your Accountability Partner

You need a solid, trustworthy, and loving Christian woman to walk with you, right beside you, through these difficult steps of escape from abuse. She must have a strong, personal relationship with Jesus Christ and be growing in that relationship. You must be able to trust her to keep everything you tell her confidential.

She will meet with you in person at least once a week to provide spiritual and emotional support. She'll be available to you 24/7 by phone. She will pray for you. She'll cry with you. She'll laugh with you. She'll share your pain. She'll encourage you and motivate you. She will not let you quit or lose heart. She will not allow you to give in to the abuser's pleas while he makes no changes. And she won't let you stop implementing your plan. She will not give up on you.

If your pastor is supportive, ask him or his wife for names of potential accountability partners. You may find a woman who has already been down the road you're on and has achieved freedom from an abusive husband. Pray that God will lead you to the right woman. He knows who she is, and He'll get the two of you together.

Family and Friends

Share the truth about your husband only with those family members and friends with whom you have an intimate relationship and whom you can trust 100 percent. They may already know about or suspect the abuse. Or they may not have a clue, because you've covered up the truth so well. Your days of lying to protect your husband are over. Your family and friends need to know what's been happening in your marriage, and they need to know now.

Abigail enlisted the support of the young men of her household (see 1 Sam. 25:14–19). And she told David the truth about Nabal (vv. 23–31). As Abigail did, as you enlist help, share the truth only with family and friends whom you are confident will understand your painful situation and support you completely. If your parents, siblings, or other family members have never supported you or have even mistreated you, don't bother to reach out to them. Tell only those who have clearly supported you and demonstrated that they understood your situation.

At this point, don't talk with your husband's family or friends. They will most likely support him and blame you.

Your family and friends can provide critical spiritual and emotional support. They can also provide essential practical support, such as babysitting, financial help or advice, assistance in finding a job, and possibly a safe place for you to live temporarily. Down the road, they may be involved in confronting your husband.

A Small Group

I urge you to join a small group of believers. You will attend alone, without your abuser. Most likely, the small group will be connected to your church. In this kind of group, you can truly connect with others. You will receive love, feedback, camaraderie, prayer, and a source of accountability. It could be a home group, a Bible study group, a men's or women's group, or a twelve-step group such as Celebrate Recovery. Just make sure it's a Christ-centered small group, one that recognizes that the "higher power" is Jesus Christ.

The power of a small group is nothing short of amazing. The individuals in your small group will become important members of your support team.

A Tough, Experienced Attorney

Find a reputable family-law attorney and consult with her in secret. You need legal guidance for financial matters, child custody, and visitation issues, as well as your rights during the separation.

When you and the kids leave your abuser, he will try everything to bring you back, including threats about the children and finances.

When he realizes you're not coming back, he'll try to destroy you financially. He'll harass and try to intimidate you. He'll attempt to drive a wedge between you and your kids. Many abusers will find an unethical attorney to do their dirty work.

You need a tough, take-no-prisoners attorney who will protect you, your kids, and your new life. Get the best possible attorney, Christian or not.

If you cannot afford an attorney, call your county and ask for free legal services.

A Tough, Experienced Christian Therapist

To move successfully through my "Escape from Abuse" plan, you'll need a wise and experienced psychological coach, someone who understands the dynamics of an abusive relationship and has guided many women through the escape process. This will be a person who can help you do three very important things:

- Figure out why you have tolerated the abuse
- Heal from your unresolved past pain
- Become an emotionally healthy woman who will stay in a marriage only when her husband treats her in a loving and respectful way

This person will be a Christian counselor. He or she may be a psychologist or a master's-level therapist. Here's the profile of the counselor you're looking for: a committed Christian who attends church weekly, whose marriage (if married) is strong and vibrant, is licensed in the mental-health field (psychology, mental health, clinical social work, or marriage and family therapy), experienced in working with abused spouses, and is a strong and assertive person who agrees with my "Escape from Abuse" plan.

To find an excellent therapist, ask your pastor or your friends, and call Focus on the Family (1-800-A-FAMILY) for referrals. You can reach out to me—I may know a therapist in your area.

It will take time to gather your team of warriors. That's okay. Start the selection process, and choose carefully. God and your human team will carry you out of your abusive relationship.

CHAPTER 13

Get Emotionally Healthy, Part One

My client's dad was abusive to her mom. He lobbed vicious criticism, sarcasm, and insults at her daily. Whenever her mom disagreed with him or brought up a topic he didn't want to discuss, he flew into a rage. There were many topics he didn't want to discuss.

He wasn't verbally abusive to my client, but he pretty much ignored her as she grew up. He offered his daughter no praise. No affection. No time together. No interest in her life. He abused her with his neglect and rejection.

For eighteen years, her dad ignored her. And for eighteen years, she watched her dad abuse her mom. All that time, she saw her mom passively take the abuse. This abuse wounded my client deeply. She assumed that this was marriage: the husband dishes out the abuse, and the wife takes it.

She married a man just like her dad. She didn't mean to. She didn't want to. But she did. The nice, kind, loving man she dated stopped being nice, kind, and loving two months after the wedding.

Just like her mom, she took the abuse and hung in there for her kids. She acted out the role of abused wife her mother had taught her. This woman carried deep wounds from her mom's choice to do nothing about the abuse, deep wounds from her dad, and deep, ongoing wounds from her abusive husband.

These wounds from her mom, dad, and husband kept her stuck in trauma. She could not get emotionally healthy enough to make her escape. She was paralyzed.

I helped her heal from her father wounds first. She relived a number of abusive memories of her dad—both verbally and in writing. When we finished with him, I helped her heal from her mother wounds. Once healed of these parental wounds, she was able to move forward with my escape plan.

Proverbs 15:13 tells us, "A glad heart makes a cheerful face, but by sorrow of heart the spirit is crushed" (ESV). What's it like to have a glad heart? You have no idea. You're not happy, and you haven't been happy for a long time. You won't be happy as long as you choose to stay with your abuser.

Your ongoing heartache is crushing your spirit. You must choose to stop tolerating abuse.

The bad news is, you are not an emotionally healthy person. You are unable, at this time, to leave your abuser. The good news is, you can become emotionally healthy and get out of the abusive relationship—if you want to.

WHO YOU ARE RIGHT NOW

Right now, you are not an independent, assertive person. You allow your abuser to control and direct your life. You allow him to tell you how to think, how to feel, what to do.

Your entire life is focused on trying to make your abuser happy while coping with his never-ending mistreatment of you. You have no identity of your own. Your identity is only what he gives you. And he gives you only abuse.

In addition, you are a martyr. Merriam-Webster defines a martyr this way: "a person who sacrifices something of great value and especially life itself for the sake of principle." You are definitely sacrificing something of great value: your life and the lives of your kids. You are giving up the wonderful plan God has for you and your children.

> *Your focus should not be about him anymore. It's about you and your kids, and the life God wants you to live.*

For what? What is the principle for which you are making this sacrifice? Changing your abusive husband? Chasing the pipe dream of a happy marriage and family? You're wasting your time. You're wasting your and your children's lives.

As long as you stay with him and tolerate his abuse, he will never change. The only way he might change—and it is a very slight possibility—is if and after you separate physically from him.

But as I have already communicated, your focus should not be about him anymore. It's about you and your kids, and the life God wants you to live.

Why do you stay with someone who is destroying you and your children? That is the big question you have to answer.

I started helping you answer this question in part 2: "Why You Stay." Now it's time for you to address the sources of your fears and the lies you tell yourself. What gives power to your fears and lies?

I know why you continue to endure abuse—unresolved pain in

your family of origin, in your personal life, and possibly in previous romantic relationships.

Who hurt you so badly that you've never been the same since that hurt? Who hurt you so badly that you think you deserve abuse? Who hurt you so badly that your self-esteem is shredded, and you believe you can't ever leave your abuser?

Your Christian therapist will help you make a list of those who harmed or traumatized you. Your therapist will help you deal with these wounds, heal from them, and become emotionally healthy.

You can become a person who will no longer tolerate abuse from anyone—a person who will have the strength, with God's help, to leave her abuser and begin a new life.

It may take four to six months in therapy to get healthy and strong. Take the time and do your work. It will be worth it.

YOUR PAST UNRESOLVED PAIN

If your father abused your mother, you are programmed to be a passive enabler, and you'll be drawn to abusive men. Your dad's abuse of your mother may have been dramatic and obvious—as in physical violence, alcoholism, or drug abuse—or it may have been vicious verbal attacks. It may have been a subtler type of abuse, such as neglect, or controlling behavior, or always having to be right.

During your childhood, your father or stepfather, your grandfather, uncle, brother, stepbrother, neighbor boy, or another male may have emotionally or sexually abused you. You may have been raped when you were a teenager or young woman.

You may have had a series of boyfriends who rejected you, controlled you, or verbally abused you. You may have allowed, perhaps because of low self-esteem, a boyfriend or boyfriends to have sex with you.

If I could talk with you for thirty minutes, I'd know exactly what in your past causes you to permit the abuse your husband dishes out. This is what your Christian professional counselor will show you. With his or her guidance, you will be able to work through your past pain and move forward as a new woman and a new wife.

YOUR KIDS AND THERAPY

Your Christian therapist will also assess your children and help make sure they are able to cope effectively with the escape process. What you tell your children, and when, about the abuse and the steps you are taking against it will depend on their ages, level of maturity, and personalities. They may already be aware of some things.

Your children need to know the truth about the abuse and what it's costing you and them.

They need to know what steps you're taking to escape it. They need to be emotionally ready before you reach the point when you confront your husband. Your Christian therapist will help you and the kids build toward becoming emotionally prepared for this final, tough-love step.

If your husband is aware that you're going for counseling, tell him it's for you and your issues. He is not invited—not yet—and you will not tell him what you are actually doing in counseling. Most likely, he'll be fine with your attending counseling alone because he's convinced you're the one with problems, and you're at fault for any marital issues.

With the help of your Christian therapist and support team, make every effort to convince your children to tell their father *nothing* about your plan to leave him. You will not tell the kids the specifics of your plan to leave until shortly before you do leave.

If one of your children accidentally gives your husband hints about your escape plan, tell your abuser: "That's a surprise. I have no plans to leave you."

That's right. You lie to him. Do not admit you are leaving—doing so would put you and the children at great risk. The safest exit plan is to take your kids and leave him in secret.

If he does find out you're leaving him, do not tell him anything about your plans. Tell your support team your abuser is aware of your intention to leave, and lean on them for safety and support. If your abuser goes into an angry, vicious, verbal attack mode, move up your timetable and leave him as soon as you can. If he threatens you with physical violence or is actually physically violent, call 911. If he is physically violent to you, have your attorney immediately file for a restraining order.

WHAT THERAPY WILL DO FOR YOU

Why is therapy so important for you? It will help you gain (at least) seven benefits:

- Find out why you were drawn to your abusive spouse
- Find out why you stay
- Identify and understand the abusive cycle
- Heal from your unresolved wounds inflicted by others and by your husband
- Build your self-esteem and confidence, both in yourself and God
- Develop a strong, healthy voice for yourself
- Get emotionally strong so you can follow my escape plan, prepare your kids to leave, get out, and handle your spouse's attacks after you leave

Remember my client from earlier in this chapter? The one with the father and mother wounds? Let's walk through the seven benefits she received from engaging in therapy with me.

Find Out Why You Were Drawn to Your Abusive Spouse

I made this clear in my explanation of her past unresolved wounds connected to her father and mother. Her unresolved father and mother wounds set her up to choose a man who would also abuse her. She recreated the same abusive relationship she had witnessed growing up.

Find Out Why You Stay

She stayed because being abused, though traumatizing, was what she was used to experiencing. Abuse was all she had known her entire life. She also stayed because she mistakenly believed it was best for her children.

Identify and Understand the Abusive Cycle

We exposed, in detail, the cycle of abuse she and her husband engaged in repeatedly, and the parallels with the cycle her parents had repeated umpteen times in front of her. Once she understood her role in the abusive cycle, she was able to stop contributing to the craziness. She was done playing the game and allowing him to do real damage to her.

Heal from Your Unresolved Wounds Inflicted by Others and by Him

I've already explained, in a basic way, how she faced these wounds and healed from them. After cleaning out her parent wounds, she cleaned out her abusive husband wounds. She told me: "A huge burden has been lifted off me. I feel like my soul has been cleansed."

Build Your Self-Esteem and Confidence Both in Yourself and God

As she did her hard work in therapy, she grew to love herself the way God loves her. She believed a truth that she had never believed before: she could, with God's power, get away from her abuser and build a new life.

Develop a Strong, Healthy Voice for Yourself

It was beautiful to watch her cast aside her old, timid, passive self and become a new, confident, assertive person. She swept away all the eggshells she'd been walking on around her abuser. She spoke her mind and didn't care about his reaction.

Get Emotionally Strong

When she started in therapy, she believed there was no way she could ever be strong enough or ready enough to leave her abuser. She did her work in the above six areas, she got strong enough to leave, and she left the abuse behind.

Her abuser is still a nasty, narcissistic, angry man who hates her. The wonderful thing is, she doesn't care. She is happy. Her kids are happy. She's out of her abusive prison, and life is good.

You, too, can get emotionally strong so you can follow my escape plan, prepare your kids to leave, get out, and handle your husband's attacks after you leave.

TROUBLE FINDING A THERAPIST?

If your abuser doesn't want you to see a therapist, see one anyway. If you have your own money (such as your own bank account), use it to see a therapist. If your abuser controls all the money, and you don't have a job with a paycheck, ask your church, your family and friends, and your small group for money to pay for therapy.

If no qualified, experienced Christian therapists practice in your area, find a godly, mature woman to help you in your emotional healing process. It could be a friend who has been abused and escaped her abuser, or a woman in a support group you attend.

If you are unable to see a therapist, I recommend my book on emotional healing, *I'm Not OK and Neither Are You—The Six Steps to Emotional Freedom*. It's a self-directed, step-by-step journey to emotional health.

To become emotionally healthy and strong enough to leave, you need to address two areas of trauma recovery: abuse inflicted by others before you met your abuser, and abuse inflicted by your abuser.

This emotional recovery work is difficult. But with God's and your team's help, you can do it. You can shed your codependency. You can stop tolerating and enabling abuse. You can build a new life of freedom for yourself and your children.

CHAPTER 14

Get Emotionally Healthy, Part Two

I t was one year ago, the day after Valentine's Day," the woman said as she sat across from me in my office. Her words came haltingly.

> We were sitting in the living room watching television. My husband asked me a question, and because I didn't hear it, I didn't answer. He flew into a rage and threw his cup against the wall. He went into a long, angry rant about how I never answer his questions. I tried to say I hadn't heard the question, but he shouted me down. He said I was either lying or, just as bad, not listening. He brought up two recent times when I had also not responded to a question.
>
> He placed himself right in front of me so I couldn't stand and leave the room. He shook his fist at me and accused me of not loving him, of being selfish and insensitive and disrespectful.

He went on for twenty minutes, cutting me off each time I tried to apologize or defend myself. He called me these awful names . . .

She listed every nasty, vile name he uttered. Her eyes showed the intense pain she felt. Then she continued:

I was stunned, scared, deeply hurt, and very frustrated. It was as if I were a trapped dog, being punished for disobeying her master. I felt like a failure, an awful wife. I thought his rant was my fault because if I had only responded to his question, he wouldn't have gotten so upset. I determined to listen better in the future.

As I tried to go to sleep a few hours later, I cried and cried. I remembered seeing the scared faces of the children as I tucked them in for the night. I know they heard every word of his rant. They must think I am a terrible wife.

There are no shortcuts in the work of trauma recovery. There is no way to skip steps or accelerate the process of healing. The only way to truly heal is to directly face the traumatic events and relive them.

God will give you the power and endurance to do the incredibly hard and painful work of trauma recovery.

God will give you the power and endurance to do the incredibly hard and painful work of trauma recovery. God will use the process of recovery to heal you, mold you, change you, and renew you. At the end of the process, you'll be much closer to Him. And you'll be able to leave your abuser.

Once you've healed from the wounds others have caused (I covered this in the previous chapter), you need to turn your attention to the wounds your abuser has caused.

TRAUMA RECOVERY STRATEGIES

While your Christian therapist will guide you in healing from the wounds of your abuser, I want to recommend two trauma recovery strategies I've found effective in my therapy.

List the Abusive Events

Go back to the beginning of your present relationship, when you first met, and make a list of the times your spouse has abused you. You won't include every abusive event—that would make too long a list—but you will list the major ones.

Pray that God will help you remember the traumatic occurrences of abuse He wants you to remember. God will spare you from recalling all of them; He knows that would be overwhelming and unnecessary.

God will bring to your mind a certain number of abusive events—seven, ten, twelve, fifteen—and these incidents will cover all the abuse you've taken from your husband.

As you list each event, write a detailed description of it. When you deal in generalities, you are avoiding the pain, and sidestepping the awful truth leads to zero healing. As much as it hurts, retelling the pain in detail leads to true healing.

From start to finish, you are reliving each abusive event: what happened just before the incident, what the abuser said and did during the event, what you said and did, where the event happened, how long the event lasted, your emotions during and after the event, what you were thinking during and after the event, all the pain and anguish you experienced, and the impact of the abuse on you and your children and others.

If you avoid the details and the pain attached to them, the trauma stays inside you—fully intact—and you remain emotionally weak. If you face the details and the pain attached to them, you'll break up the trauma, and it will begin to leave you. And then you'll become emotionally stronger.

Once you've written the account of the abusive events, you'll read it to your therapist and talk through each event. You'll also read it to your accountability partner. Let my client's description at the beginning of this chapter be an example of how you'll need to describe the abuse you've suffered so you can find healing.

As my client and I worked through the abuse she'd suffered from her husband, it was hard to convince her that her husband's rant and abuse were not her fault. I had her talk through a half dozen of his recent rants so she could see that her behavior had nothing to do with his abusive monologues. I then listed each back to her:

> "You were just sitting at the kitchen table . . . and he ranted."
> "You accidentally bumped his arm . . . and he ranted."
> "You cried at the end of the movie . . . and he ranted."
> "You laughed at his friend's joke . . . and he ranted."
> "You smiled at the waiter . . . and he ranted."
> "You didn't hear his question . . . and he ranted."

She began to realize that there was no connection between what she did or said and his nasty, verbally abusive rants. He verbally abused her because of his own sin and dysfunction. He ranted because he wanted to control her and make her suffer. I told her, "You could hand him a million dollars and offer to make love to him all night, and he might still go into a rant."

By directly facing these abusive memories, you will see that none of the abuse you have suffered is your fault. Every single abusive event is completely the fault of your abuser.

List All Your Losses

Another strategy is to write down all the losses you've suffered because of living with your abuser. To this point, you've coped by living in denial, not admitting these losses to yourself or anyone else.

It's time to drop the denial act and honestly acknowledge the losses you've allowed your abuser to inflict on you. This exercise will hurt you, but it's a good, healthy hurt.

By putting on paper your losses and reading them to your therapist and your accountability partner, you'll move past denying the abuse and into reality. You'll realize with sickening clarity what living with your abuser has cost you. If you do this, you'll take significant steps toward healing, getting stronger, and being motivated to leave.

As you did with the abusive events, you'll describe each loss in detail: what the abuser has done to cause the loss, the pain of the loss, your emotions connected to the loss, the impact of the loss on your life and the lives of others, and how you plan to reverse the process and *get back* what was taken from you.

For an example of what this looks like, consider this wife's list of losses:

Dave, here's what I've lost because of living with my abuser.
I've lost my:
happiness
joy
peace
sanity

self-esteem
self-confidence
independence
identity
career
energy and drive
parents and siblings
physical health
close connection to God
friends
dignity
self-respect
the respect and love of my children

I asked this abused woman to write down and talk through, in detail, each loss on her list. Here's what she came up with for one of these losses:

Okay, I've lost my self-esteem. I used to like myself and believe I had talents and abilities. I thought I was physically attractive. I thought I was smart, organized, a good cook, and a good housekeeper. I thought I was a good worker, and I was proud of my career. Most important, I thought I was a good mom. I don't believe any of that anymore. My husband, my abuser, has convinced me that I'm worthless. His regular criticism in every area has devastated my positive view of myself. He's called me fat, stupid, ignorant, a poor organizer, a lazy cook and housekeeper, and a mediocre employee whose job doesn't bring in enough money.

Most painful of all have been his criticisms of my mothering. I don't spend enough time with the children, I spend too much time with them, I'm not hard enough on them, I'm too hard on them, I don't do enough to help them succeed in school, I don't support the decisions he makes as a father. All his criticism has hurt me and made me feel like a pitiful loser. I feel inadequate, unworthy, and hopeless. I live every day waiting to make more mistakes he will point out.

I'm physically exhausted, and don't work on my appearance. I spend way too much time trying to please him. I don't feel like I'm doing anything well. I'm not a good wife, not a good mom, not a good worker, not a good Christian, not a good anything. I want desperately to get my self-esteem back. I long to be the person I once was, the person who liked herself.

After she read the details of her loss, she looked up at me. "I can see how my abuser's criticism has shredded my view of myself and turned it all negative. He's a liar, isn't he? He's wrong about me, isn't he?"

"He's absolutely, totally, 100 percent wrong about you!" I told her. "He always has been, and chances are he always will be. You're going to get your self-esteem back. You're going to get your confidence back. You're going to get your dignity back. You're going to see yourself the way God sees you, and God knows you better than anyone."

I also instructed this woman to write down the losses her children had suffered because of their abusive father. Not surprisingly, many of her losses were also on the list of her children's losses.

I asked her to read and talk about each of her children's losses too. This was brutal and painful for her to do, but also very self-discovering—and healing for her.

Listing abusive events and listing losses are just two strategies that can help you become emotionally healthy. Your therapist will have many more strategies to guide you in your journey of healing, recovery, escape from your abuser, and building your new life.

CHAPTER 15

Get Financially Healthy

When you leave your abuser—or before, if he figures out you are planning to leave him—he will immediately use money to punish you. He'll try to break you financially in order to force you to give up your escape plan and stay with him.

After you have left, and your unrepentant abuser realizes you're not coming back, he'll use his money—and he believes the money is all his—to destroy you.

Here's what he'll do:

He'll cut you off from the money.

He'll cancel your credit, debit, and ATM cards.

He'll put all the money into his own personal accounts.

He'll steal money that is partly in your name and hide it in secret accounts or send it to his family members.

He'll stall in the legal process to wear you down while your money supply diminishes.

He'll lower his income to cheat you out of money.

He'll spend huge sums on attorneys, so there will be little or
nothing left.

He'll take you back to court to get his child support and
alimony payments reduced.

He'll fight you for custody of the children so he will not have
to pay child support.

He'll be chronically late with his child support and alimony
payments.

You'll need money for your attorney, your Christian therapist,
the place you live, and all your living expenses. Eventually you may
get money from your spouse in a legal separation (or a divorce, if
it comes to that), but he will stall, pay you as little as possible, and
be late with his payments.

You need a savings war chest and a steady source of income
that will support you and the children.

Here are the healthy financial steps I want you to take before
you leave your abuser.

FIND OUT WHERE THE MONEY IS,
AND GET YOUR NAME ON IT

Find all your financial records: tax returns for the last three years,
and documents of your savings and checking bank accounts, credit
union accounts, 401(k) accounts, and retirement accounts. Make
copies of these, and keep them in a safe, secure place.

You need to know exactly what your husband earns as stated
on the copy of a payroll check or statement. You need to know
exactly where all the money is deposited. You will need to have
a complete picture of your assets and liabilities. Record the exact
amount of debt the two of you have. Find out where all monies

are invested, who is doing the investing, and how your investments are doing.

There is probably a financial expert in your church who can guide you in this money area. If you have a financial advisor, meet with him privately and have him or her fill you in on your total financial portfolio. Ask him not to tell your husband about the meeting. If he can't or won't do that, so be it.

If your abuser learns that you're getting all this financial information—and he probably will— make no apology.

Tell your husband what you are doing, and have the meeting with the advisor anyway.

If your abuser learns that you're getting all this financial information—and he probably will—make no apology. Tell him because you are his wife, you want to know all about the finances so you can be prepared in case he is disabled or dies.

Get your name on all the assets: car(s), house(s), bank, retirement and investment accounts, insurance policies—including disability insurance—and all properties. Make sure there is no debt in your name only.

If he fights you on these financial moves—and he certainly will—your attorney will take the action necessary to protect you in the money arena.

LEAN ON YOUR ATTORNEY

Meet with your tough, knuckle-and-skull-fighting family-law attorney and ask him what he can do legally to give you financial protection. How can you get your name on all the assets? How much money can you take just before you leave your abuser? How do you apply for child support and temporary financial support, and what amount of that can you expect during the separation?

A good attorney will know precisely how to advise you in the financial area. It's his or her job to protect you and your kids.

START YOUR OWN PERSONAL, SECRET BANK ACCOUNT

Begin putting money into a secret bank account that's in your name only. If you have a job outside the home, put as much money in that account as possible from each paycheck. If you don't work outside the home, squirrel away as much as you can in this account.

The amounts you put into this account will have to be small, so he will not notice.

Also, ask your support system, especially family and friends, for donations to this private account.

This is your escape war chest.

GET A JOB

If you don't have a job, get one. Reach out to all your contacts, and pray God gives you a job that will eventually support you and your kids. Get this job before you leave your abuser. You need money for your war chest and for your living expenses after you've left.

Tell your husband you want a job so you can contribute to the family support, so you can buy extra things you want, and so you can fulfill your potential as a person. He won't like it, but he can't stop you from doing it.

He'll most likely closely watch the money you make, so at least half of it may have to go into a joint account. Take at least half of each paycheck and put it into your secret account. If he asks about this missing money, tell him this money is to buy things for yourself.

If he demands that you deposit your entire paycheck into a joint account, you calmly refuse. You have to take a stand on this issue because you need this money for your escape war chest.

GET EDUCATION AND TRAINING

If you need more or specific education or some kind of technical training in order to get a decent job, get it. If he refuses to pay for it, ask your family, friends, and church for the funds. Your community may have a women's center that will provide job training and guidance.

HOW YOUR FINANCES
MAY AFFECT YOUR CHILDREN

Getting more education and/or getting a job may mean a big change in your kids' schooling. You may have to stop homeschooling. You may have to pull them out of private school. It's likely your kids will have to attend public school.

These are real sacrifices, but keep this in mind: having the money to escape your abuser is more important than your children being homeschooled or attending private school. As you begin this escape preparation, pray for God to protect your kids throughout this process.

Your education, training, and eventual job will also mean you'll have less time with your kids. That's reality. You may not be able to drop them off at school or pick them up. You may not be able to transport them to their activities.

Lean on your support team for help in these areas. If you have to pay an older teen or young adult to help with the kids, do it. If you have to use day care, do it.

Again, taking all these steps is more important than staying with your abuser and watching him damage your kids.

These difficult steps will take time and energy. You may have to work at your emotional health to be strong enough to take these financial actions. It will take time, but you will be able to follow these money steps. They are vital to your successful escape.

Recently, I worked with a wife who was finally ready to prepare to leave her abusive husband. She hadn't worked outside the home for years. She had three kids she homeschooled.

At the beginning of her escape process, she felt overwhelmed and believed she could never take these financial steps.

I told her, "I have helped many wives in your situation. You *can* take these steps."

Though it took eight months, she reached the point where she could leave her abuser and be financially secure. She added her name on key assets. She followed her attorney's advice regarding what money she could take when she left. She opened her own personal, secret bank account. She found a decent job.

She had to put her kids in public school. That was a painful, but necessary decision. Her kids understood this decision and supported it. They wanted to get away from their abusive dad too.

This woman is not rich. In fact, she and the kids are just able to pay the bills. But they are rich in peace of mind, happiness, and security.

I hope you've decided to follow my plan just as this woman did so you can reach that same happy destination. Now we need to talk about how to get your precious children ready for your escape.

CHAPTER 16

Get Your Kids Ready to Leave, Part One

My client, who for the previous three months had worked hard on her codependency and her wounds, told me: "I'm feeling a lot stronger. I'm done putting up with his abuse. I know it's best for me and my kids to leave him. I thought I was protecting my kids by staying. I know now that's not true. But I'm afraid my kids aren't ready to leave. I don't want to hurt them or traumatize them by taking them out of the home."

I told her what I've told thousands of abused moms: "Of course you are worried about your children. Your worries are completely valid. Leaving will be hard on them, but it will give them their best opportunity to heal from the abuse and develop into godly, happy adults. We won't take any chances with your precious kids and their emotional well-being. I will show you how to get your kids ready to leave. You won't leave until you are confident they are fully prepared to go with you."

You're out of denial, and you know you have to leave your abuser. You're getting closer to God. You're gathering your support team. You're working hard on your emotional health. You're getting your financial life in order.

Now it's time to focus on getting your children ready to leave your abuser. (And, frankly, he's their abuser, too.)

Because you want the best for your children, getting them ready to leave is important for them. Knowing you have done all you can to prepare them to leave is also important for you. You can't leave until you know *they're* ready to leave.

GAIN YOUR CHILDREN'S RESPECT

You have allowed—for years—your abuser to blatantly disrespect you. You've bitten your tongue, swallowed your feelings, and stifled your opinions a million times. The abuse and your nonreactions have occurred many times in front of your kids.

Because of your children's ringside seat to your passive acceptance of his abuse, they have no respect for you. Because your kids don't respect you, they won't listen to you. They won't trust you to keep them safe. They will side with the abuser.

You can't afford any longer for your kids to see you as the weaker—or even guilty—spouse. If they see you treated like a doormat, they will treat you like a doormat too. Your children will ignore everything you express—your feelings, your opinions, your teachings, and biblical truths.

In the awful, mixed-up world created by abuse in your marriage, your kids will respect the abuser. He is the one speaking with authority; you are the one who appears guilty because you will not stand up to him. They will listen to what he has to say. They might be scared of him, but they'll listen to him. They'll believe his lies—about you, about him, and about everything else.

Before you leave, you *must* have your children's respect.

SPEAK UP IN ONE-WAY STATEMENTS IN FRONT OF THE KIDS

Every time—*every* time—your abuser mistreats you in front of the children, immediately make a short and clear statement to him naming the mistreatment for what it is, and how you feel about it.

These are *one-way* statements. You verbalize them with no expectation of or desire for a response from your abuser. You're not making these statements to gain his respect. You are making these statements to gain your children's respect and let them hear the truth about what happened:

"That comment was mean and hurtful."
"I'm angry that you just criticized my weight."
"What you said is not true."
"It's rude and disrespectful of you to dismiss my opinion."
"That behavior is selfish and hurtful."

You should not say these things in a nasty way. That's important, because you don't want to act like him. The children must see a difference. Just be firm and honest. Of course, he will not like it when you make these statements. He'll say something mean and sarcastic after your one-way statement. When he does, either ignore him or say, "What I said still stands."

Your brief statements of truth show your children that what he's saying and doing is wrong and sinful. If you don't point that

> *Be careful not to degrade him or speak in a deliberately unkind manner. Just tell the truth.*

out, your kids won't realize it's wrong. Plus, your statements will begin to generate respect from your children.

When your abuser mistreats the kids in your presence, quickly step in to protect them. This will limit the damage and show them that you "have their back" when their dad is mean.

DEBRIEF WITH YOUR KIDS

After an abusive event, whether your spouse has abused you or one of your kids, talk to your children in private about what happened. Explain to each child how Dad's *behavior* was wrong and hurtful. Be careful not to degrade him or speak in a deliberately unkind manner. Just tell the truth.

Also, teach each child the proper and biblical way to treat a person. Simply state your feelings; do *not* attack the person.

Again and again, your message to the children will be: *Dad is doing things that are wrong; the Bible is right.*

Quote Joshua 24:15 to your children over and over again: "If serving the LORD seems undesirable to you, then choose for yourselves this day whom you will serve. . . . As for me and my household, we will serve the LORD" (NIV).

Tell your kids: "Dad can choose to do and say whatever he wants. But we can choose to serve the Lord and do and say what He wants."

SET BOUNDARIES AND DISCIPLINE YOUR KIDS

A key way to earn your children's respect is by being a solid, healthy disciplinarian. Establish reasonable behavior standards and practical rewards and consequences. When a child chooses to obey a behavior standard, he chooses to get a reward. When a child chooses to disobey a behavior standard, he chooses to get a consequence.

My book on parenting, *Parenting Is Hard and Then You Die*, will help you develop and implement an effective strategy of discipline. (As you are beginning to realize, I have a book for everything.)

When your abuser overrides one of your parenting decisions, use a one-way statement in the children's presence to make your position clear, and to emphasize that you think he is wrong. For instance, "I think staying up an extra hour is a mistake, since you have school exams tomorrow. Because this is your father's idea, he can do the bedtime routine tonight. Good night." Later, in private, tell the kids in more detail why you believe Dad made the wrong decision.

When your abuser is not around, discipline the children the way you believe is right.

CHAPTER 17

Get Your Kids Ready to Leave, Part Two

Here's what happened when one woman took the time to prepare her kids for leaving. When she first talked with me, this wife and mom looked sad and tired.

"Can you help me manage my husband's abusive behavior?" she asked. "I won't leave him because I have two kids."

"No, I can't help you with that," I told her. "What I can do is help you and your kids leave your abuser."

After I had convinced her that leaving was the best—and the biblical—option, we focused on her emotional health. Once she was strong enough, we turned our attention to getting her kids ready to leave.

It took her a year and a half to leave her abuser. She spent much of that time preparing her kids for the escape. She followed all the action steps in the previous two chapters. And it wasn't easy.

Her younger son was all for leaving. He was close to her and hated the abuse his mom was suffering. He put up no resistance to the preparation steps.

Her teenage daughter was a different story. She was closer to her dad and had taken on the characteristics of a codependent enabler. She had learned from her mother how to live in denial, justifying her dad's abusive words and behavior.

This daughter was opposed to leaving her dad. She fought her mother's escape plan tooth and nail. After six months of therapy and watching her mom grow into an assertive, confident woman, she agreed that leaving was the right thing to do.

The three of them—mom, son, and daughter—were in my office two months after leaving the abuser. I asked the kids how they felt about getting out.

"It's a huge relief," the boy answered. "I wanted Mom to stop putting up with Dad's anger and nasty words. He treated her like dirt. It wasn't easy leaving, and it's not easy now, but I'm a lot happier. I think we're all a lot happier."

The girl reported: "I put up a big fight about leaving. I was so used to the abuse, I didn't see it as abuse. I always excused Dad's behavior, just like Mom did for years. I believed leaving would be betraying him. When I realized the damage he was doing to all of us, I knew we had to leave. Like my brother said, it's not easy living on our own. But, man, is it better! I can sleep at night. I don't have to worry about his next explosion. Life is good."

You can do several more things to make it easier for your kids when you leave your abuser.

KEEP YOUR CHILDREN IN CHURCH

Do everything in your power to keep your kids in church every week. Smaller kids need a solid children's ministry. Teenagers need a solid youth ministry. If your church doesn't have these programs, find one that does.

In these church programs, your children will be taught the Bible. They will grow spiritually and learn that God is there for them always.

They will make quality friends, and you will too, including other parents. By being involved in church, your kids will have godly adult role models.

As your kids spend time with godly married couples, they will see how a man is supposed to treat his wife.

Your abuser may not like you or the kids attending church. Too bad. You and the kids are going. If he doesn't want to go, that's fine. You don't care. It's actually a little break from him and his abuse.

LOOK FOR GODLY ADULT ROLE MODELS

Your kids need godly men and women to look up to and admire. Many of these godly adults will be in your church: your pastor, an associate pastor, the worship pastor, the youth pastor, Sunday school teachers, or husbands and wives of your friends.

Christian coaches, teachers, leaders of the children's activities and interests, neighbors, and family members can also serve as potential models.

Since your marriage is dysfunctional, expose your kids to God-honoring, healthy, loving marriages. As your kids spend time with godly married couples, they will see how a man is supposed to treat his wife.

One abused wife I was counseling in my office had a thirteen-year-old son. She was concerned that leaving his father would harm him. "*Not* leaving your husband will harm your son," I told her. "Leaving this abusive situation will save your son and give him a far better chance to grow into a godly young man."

Godly adult role models for your kids are out there. And they are closer than you think.

I encouraged her to reach out to her church's youth pastor. She explained to him the abuse and her plan to leave. And she asked him to come alongside her son to provide support, love, and mentoring, and to be a godly male role model.

The youth pastor, who was a younger man, came through and built a strong relationship with her teenage son. This bond helped the son deal with the painful emotions and adjustment connected with the escape process. This wife left her abuser, and the youth pastor stayed close to her son for several critical years.

Godly adult role models for your kids are out there. And they are closer than you think. Wherever they are—your church, your family, your kids' schools, the leaders of your kids' activities and sports, or your neighborhood—God will lead you to them.

BUILD YOUR KIDS' SPIRITUAL LIVES

Church and godly role models are important, but they are not enough. At least once a week, lead a family devotional time with your children. Read a brief, practical devotion, and apply it to your life and to each of their lives. Close these times by having each person pray for the person on his or her right.

Teach each child how to do a daily devotional and prayer time with God. At the end of each day, spend a few minutes alone with each child. Ask how the day went, be sure to *listen* attentively, and pray for him or her.

God can use this escape process to strengthen your children's spiritual lives. Pray diligently for this. God hears your prayers.

KEEP YOUR KIDS IN HEALTHY ACTIVITIES

Do your best to keep each of your children in one fun, healthy activity: a school sport, a community sports league, martial arts, dance, theater, chorus, playing a musical instrument, or something else. This activity will build your children's self-esteem and confidence. It's a stimulating distraction from the tense, often-frightening atmosphere at home, and it's a good social and physical outlet.

If you can't transport them to their activities, ask your support team for help.

DIRECT PREPARATION FOR YOUR ESCAPE

After a period of some months, maybe as much as a year, you'll be emotionally and financially ready to leave your abuser. During this period, you'll have initiated most of these steps to prepare your kids to leave with you.

Once you're at this stage of the plan, it's time to talk to your children directly and specifically about leaving.

BE HONEST ABOUT THE ABUSE

Gather your children and tell them how their dad has abused you over the years. They have witnessed many events of abuse, but have not, until recently, realized his behavior was abusive, or that what was happening does not happen in other homes. Since you have been answering abuse with your one-way statements, and since you have been debriefing your children, they now have a better picture of the abusive behavior.

Talk about the highlights of the abusive events your children have witnessed, and label these events as abuse. Then describe abusive episodes that they haven't witnessed. Do not give every detail, but tell them the types of things their father has said and done to you. For example, "Last summer, he locked me in the bathroom and wouldn't let me out until I agreed to cook him a special meal." "Remember the anniversary trip the two of us took two years ago? Your father spent hours gambling, lost big, and that's why we had to come home early." "Many, many times your father has told me I'm fat, ugly, and stupid, and that I'm lucky he stays with me."

Use age-appropriate truth. Go from the general to the specific. Encourage them to vent emotions and ask questions. Your Christian therapist will be invaluable in helping you know what to say and how to say it.

Own your responsibility for tolerating Dad's abuse for so long. But make it clear that your passive tolerance is over.

Your kids need to know why you are leaving their father. Tell them that the reason is his abuse and his decision to not stop it. Let the kids know you have asked, begged, and pleaded with him repeatedly to end the abuse. Let them know all the attempts you've made over the years to get him to quit: books, seminars, talking to pastors, praying, counseling.

You will tell the kids that they can still have a relationship with their dad, but you want them to know the truth about how he treats you.

PROVIDE BIBLICAL SUPPORT FOR LEAVING

Tell your kids that leaving an abuser is biblical. You would not leave unless God was clear in the Bible that because of the abuse, it is the right thing to do. Read the kids the story of Abigail and Nabal, and tell them you are Abigail. But let the emphasis be on your hurting so much and the need for release. Let them see and feel that.

> *Tell your children that you are separating from their dad with hope for reuniting the family.*

Tell them that if you stay, the bad words, bad behavior, and the hurt you are receiving at the hands of their father will destroy you. Tell your children that if you stay, they will be seriously harmed in the same ways. *Tell them that if you stay, their dad will never change,* and that he might change only if you leave.

Tell them the Bible teaches, in Matthew 18:15–17 and Titus 3:10–11, that it's necessary to separate from a sinner who refuses to say he is doing wrong, repent, and then change. Tell them the separation will protect you and them.

Tell your children that you are separating from their dad with hope for reuniting the family. Explain to them that this will give their dad the best chance to repent, stop the abuse, and become a godly man, husband, and father.

GET THE KIDS READY FOR DAD'S REACTION

Ask the kids not to tell their father of your secret plan to leave him. Tell them you believe the safest and best plan is to leave, with them, in a sudden and secret way. The main reason for this secrecy is that you believe his reaction can't be predicted, but you fear it will be volatile and angry. The second reason is that he will do whatever he can to stop you from leaving, and you are determined to leave.

Talk to your kids about the various reactions their father will likely have to your escape:

> He'll blame you for leaving.
>
> He'll blame the children for leaving.
>
> He'll lie about you and smear your character, falsely accusing you of bad behavior.
>
> He'll accuse you of having an affair.
>
> He'll accuse you of being a liar and a deceiver.
>
> He'll tell everyone you are crazy and mentally unstable.
>
> He'll say you're a terrible person and that leaving is a sin.
>
> He'll try to force the children to choose him over you and to choose to live with him only.
>
> He'll mistreat them, reject them, and cut them off if they don't completely side with him.
>
> He'll try to buy their loyalty with gifts.
>
> He will cut you and them off financially.
>
> He'll get church leaders and friends to side with him, and he'll ask them to persuade you and the children to come back.

PAINT A PICTURE OF SEPARATION

Talk to the kids about what separation will look like. Talk about the schedule, school, transportation, their activities, and how you will ask your support team to help with all of these issues.

Let them know you'll try to work out a reasonable schedule for the time they'll be with you and with their dad. Tell them that a fifty-fifty split of their time is probably what will happen.

Tell them that their dad will probably make promises to them and not deliver. He may not show up to get them, or he'll show up late to get them. He might keep them longer than the agreed-upon time. He'll ask them all kinds of questions about you and what you are doing. Tell them they do not have to answer these questions.

Again, lean heavily on your Christian therapist as you prepare your kids to leave. She'll advise you about what to say to them, and how and when to say it. She will work with each child in the preparation process.

I know this is beyond brutally tough. I have lived it with individuals time after time over the years.

I know, too, that one of the central reasons you have stayed with your abuser is to avoid all the confusion, pain, and trauma your kids will experience when you leave.

I have said this before, and I will say it again: *By staying, you subject your kids to never-ending pain and trauma.* By staying, you do not prevent hurt from happening in their lives, you only make the hurt and sadness last longer.

But by leaving the abusive relationship, you give your children a chance to stop the wounds and the harm. You give them a chance to heal and recover. And this is vitally important: by escaping the abuse, you'll help your kids deal much more effectively with their abusive father—perhaps over a lifetime.

If you plan your move and take this step to prepare your children, they will not shockingly and suddenly have their lives turned upside down.

By staying, you give your kids no chance. By leaving, you are following the Bible, and you are giving your children what God wants them to have and what they deserve: an opportunity—a very good opportunity—to live godly, healthy lives.

CHAPTER 18

Get Away from Your Abuser

You are finally ready to leave. You've prepared your kids to leave. It's taken months—maybe a year or more—and you have worked hard on the steps of my escape plan. After you've spent months building a boat from scratch, there comes a point when all the work is done and it's time to launch the boat. You need to get the boat in the water and motor away from shore.

I've done my best to show you that you are on solid biblical ground for your choice to leave your abuser. You're not leaving a decent husband who has made some mistakes. You're not leaving a husband who makes you unhappy at times. You are leaving an abusive, unloving husband who refuses to stop his evil, destructive, God-dishonoring behavior.

Ideally, move out when your abuser is not home. A secret move is easier and safer.

Getting out will be ugly. It will be messy. It will be an extremely difficult, painful road. But it's time to go. It's the right thing to do.

Now here's what to do next.

NO DIRECT CONTACT FOR ONE MONTH

With the help of your support team, move with your kids into your new place. Ideally, move out when your abuser is not home. A secret move is easier and safer. If he finds out about the move, surround yourself with your support team members, and move out anyway as planned.

After you've moved, go silent for one full month. Have no direct communication with your abuser. You need this time to get settled in your new home and to give you and your kids time to adjust.

Before your abuser discovers you're gone, take whatever money you can legally remove from joint accounts and deposit it in an account only you can access. Once you have moved, have your attorney take the legal actions necessary to protect you financially. These actions may include filing for legal separation and/or temporary support. Your attorney will know the legal steps to take.

Do not tell your spouse your new address. He'll find out eventually, but you want to delay this as long as possible. He is not welcome in your new home. Even after he knows where you are living, do not allow him to pick up the kids there. For drop-off and pick-up locations, use a neutral and public place such as a parking lot, a park, or a mall.

If you've chosen a new church, start attending it with your kids. When your husband has the kids, he can take them to the church he attends.

HAVE PERSONAL PROTECTION

Get some form of personal protection. The first few months are the most dangerous. Your abuser's humiliation and loss of control could push him into physical violence. If your husband has hit you in the past, he's almost certainly going to come after you physically.

Even if he has never been physically violent with you, your leaving him could easily cause him to cross the line.

It's far better to be prepared for violence than to hope and pray it won't happen.

Get a Taser or pepper spray. If your abuser has a serious anger issue, consider purchasing a handgun and applying for a concealed weapon permit.

> *Protection begins with this mindset: I will not be a victim anymore.*

A concealed weapon permit will take time—several months or more—to secure. You'll also need to take classes and submit an application. If you believe you need a handgun, start this process well before you leave.

If your abuser is a violent man, alert the police department to your escape plan. This way at least you are on record.

It's vital that you make a plan to protect yourself and your children. Protection begins with this mindset: *I will not be a victim anymore.* Even Jesus instructed His disciples to buy a sword for protection (see Luke 22:36).

In this area of protection, I turned to a close Christian friend for his expertise. If you decide to buy a firearm, here is what he recommends: "We don't learn to drive by buying a car. There is a process. We don't learn self-defense by buying a firearm and putting it in a drawer. Training is important. There are local classes that teach handgun safety and use. Call your sheriff's office for the names and locations of shooting ranges and classes. Don't google these ranges or classes, because your abuser may be spying on your internet use."

In the month of no contact after you leave, here are some more actions you need to take. Deactivate the GPS on your phone and your car. Some abusers are stalkers, so you need to be vigilant and always aware of your surroundings. Create a new email account. Change all your passwords. Set up two-factor authentication on electronic accounts. Get a new cell phone number. Consider subscribing to credit monitoring. Ask your attorney for strategies to protect yourself in this digital world.

COMMUNICATE THROUGH YOUR ATTORNEY AND YOUR SUPPORT TEAM

For at least the first month, communicate with your spouse only through others. As indicated previously, your attorney will send him the proper legal papers. Have one of your support team members contact him with this message: "She's done with you. Respect her privacy. All she wants is to work out a schedule for when you will see the kids."

With your attorney, you will develop a schedule for his time with the children. The schedule must be fair and reasonable for him in order to protect your custody rights. Your attorney or another team member will send him this proposed schedule.

The time-with-the-children agreement will depend on a number of factors, including your husband's work and travel schedule. It must follow the guidelines of your state. Many states and courts mandate a fifty-fifty split of child custody, so this may be what you propose.

Your attorney and your designated support team member will work out this agreement regarding the children's time with your abuser.

YOUR ABUSER'S REACTION

Your abuser's reaction to your departure will be revealing. It will reveal his character and his feelings for you.

The classic and most common reaction is shock and a tearful, emotional attempt to get you to come right back. He'll act confused; he'll even say he's sorry. He'll get a bunch of church leaders, friends, family members, and neighbors to contact you on his behalf. Ignore them all. You don't have the time or energy to tell all these people the entire story.

When you don't respond to him, and he realizes you're not coming back, he'll move into full-blown attack mode. He'll engage in all the nasty, abusive behaviors I mentioned in the previous chapter—and more.

You and the kids leaving him will humiliate him. It will make him look bad, and for him, image is everything. To repair his image and punish you, he'll go after you with a vengeance.

He'll mount a massive public relations campaign to discredit you and destroy your reputation. He'll claim that *you* are the abusive one, and your sudden escape proves that.

He'll say—to anyone who will listen—that you have abused him for years. He'll accuse *you* of doing all the things he did to precipitate your leaving him and of which you are accusing *him*.

He will play the poor, traumatized victim. "How could you leave without warning?" he'll say. "This is so terribly hard on me—and undeserved!"

He's a master liar, so he'll be successful and win the public-relations battle with many people. So be it. Expect and accept this. You know the truth, your support team knows the truth, and God knows the truth.

Though you do not need it, his vicious reaction simply confirms that you have done the right thing by leaving.

TAKE COURAGE: YOU AREN'T ALONE

I want to encourage you and let you know you aren't alone in this situation. Other spouses have been where you are, and they've successfully escaped from their abuser using my plan. Hear what a few of these spouses have to say:

> Leaving my abuser was the hardest thing I've ever done. Right up to the day I left, I agonized over whether it was the right thing to do. The peace and joy I feel now is God's confirmation that leaving *was* the right thing.

> From the day I left him, my abuser went into attack mode. He smeared my character to anyone who would listen. He even got some of my family members to turn on me. He doesn't realize that these hateful actions have further convinced me that I had to leave him.

> He moaned and cried and begged for ten days after I left. When that didn't work, he filed divorce papers and threatened to ruin me financially. He threatened to take my kids from me. Thank God I had my job, my own bank account, and my attorney.

I have to admit, I never thought I would have the guts or the ability to leave my wife. Despite her constant verbal abuse and physical violence and affairs, I figured I had to stay with her and take it. When I realized the damage she was doing to our kids, I knew I had to get out. Since we left, she's no different. She's already shacked up with her next victim. But the kids and I are different. And in a very good way. We're happy and safe for the first time in fifteen years. If I can get out, anyone can get out.

Even if your abuser maintains a repentant, apologetic, and humble stance for the first month, take it with a grain of salt. Actually, a half-grain of salt.

Do not respond, even if he has a good reaction. He has a long way to go if he wants you back.

PART 5

Give Your Abuser a Chance

CHAPTER 19

"Here's How You Win Me Back"

My client came to see me one month after she left her abuser. She had spent this month putting her new life in order: getting her finances set with her attorney's help, settling into her new home, getting the kids' school and activity schedule in place, organizing her support team to help with babysitting and transportation of her kids, helping the kids deal with their father's reaction with their therapist's guidance, creating a new email account and new cell phone number, changing all her passwords . . .

She had not had any contact with her abuser during this month, as per my instructions. He had started out with tears and desperation and moved to rage and harsh criticism of her. Predictably, he was blaming her for the awful betrayal of leaving him. He failed to mention his abusive behavior that caused her departure.

"Well, so far so good," she told me. "I can't quite believe I left him. I'm glad I did, but I want to make sure I follow the Bible in what I do now."

"You have followed the Bible by leaving him," I assured her. "I want you to continue to follow the Bible now that you are away from him."

It's been one month since you left your abuser. No matter what his behavior has been during this month, it's now time to "Matthew 18" him.

I refer to Matthew 18:15–17, where Jesus lays out in detail how to confront someone who has sinned against you:

> If your brother sins, go and show him his fault in private; if he listens to you, you have gained your brother. But if he does not listen to you, take one or two more with you, so that on the testimony of two or three witnesses every matter may be confirmed. And if he refuses to listen to them, tell it to the church; and if he refuses to listen even to the church, he is to be to you as a Gentile and a tax collector.

God will honor you for following Jesus' teaching on how to confront your abuser. These steps of confrontation give your abuser his best chance to repent. By following Jesus' directions, you'll show your children that you are giving their dad every opportunity to change. And finally, you should follow the Matthew 18 instructions because you know that, before God, you've done everything possible to motivate your abuser to get into recovery and to save your marriage and family.

If he wants to win you back, then he needs to make some serious changes—and you set the requirements for those.

If he wants to win you back, then he needs to make some serious changes—and you set the requirements for those. He no longer can dictate the terms of your relationship. Here's how you confront him.

YOUR LIST OF REQUIREMENTS

To actually put Matthew 18 into action, follow this plan. At the end of this first *month* of separation, through one of your support team members, give your abuser a list of actions he must carry out if he wants you back. The list is the first step in the Matthew 18 process.

Your support team member can deliver this list to your spouse in person, by email, or via regular mail. You do not meet with your abuser privately to present this list. Three reasons for this: (1) you have asked him privately a million times to make changes, and he has refused; (2) using someone else sends the message you want to send to him: *I'm done with you*; (3) it's not safe—emotionally and maybe physically—to meet with him one on one.

With the list, your support team member will communicate this message: "Your wife is done. She doesn't want you back. If you want to win her back, your only chance—and it's a very small chance—is to carry out every item on this list. When you're ready, let me know whether or not you intend to complete the list. I'll pass your response on to your wife.

"Your wife may decide to add to this list or change the list at any time. This isn't about your marriage anymore. This is about you and your relationship with God. This is your chance to confess, repent, change, and become a godly man."

After delivering the list and this brief message, your support team member ends the contact. That person will not share any other information about you or the kids. Of course, your team member will let you know how your abuser reacted to receiving the list.

This is the list he needs to follow:

1. You will see a Christian licensed therapist once a week for a minimum of six months. You will find out why you have been abusive to me, and with your therapist, you will begin a plan of recovery. You will learn how not to be selfish. You will learn how to love me and meet my needs. You will learn how to be a godly man and husband and father. You'll sign a release allowing me, if I choose, to get updates from your therapist on your progress.

2. As part of your individual therapy, you will write a complete history of how you have abused me. This history will be written in detail, from the beginning of our relationship until the day I left you. You will include any serious sins you've committed that I don't know about. You will completely and fully own the responsibility for your abusive behavior and for my leaving you because of it. You will send this document to me via my designated representative within the next three months [*give the date*].

3. You will tell the truth of how you have abused me to your pastor, your church leaders, your family, my family, and our children. If you've lied to others and slandered me, you will admit your lies and state the truth. After you've told the truth to these persons, you'll ask each of them to call me and tell me what you said to them. For those who are local, you'll talk to them in person. You'll also talk to these individuals within the next three months.

4. You will join a Celebrate Recovery group and stay in the group until you've completed an entire step study.

5. You will work very hard to grow spiritually by taking these steps:
    - Attend church every week
    - Step down from any position(s) of leadership and service within the church
    - Join a small group Bible study (and tell the group about your abusive behavior)
    - Meet weekly with a godly man for spiritual coaching
    - Engage in a daily quiet time with prayer and Bible reading
6. Find one godly man who will hold you accountable in your therapy process, your spiritual process, and regarding all the actions on this list. This could be the same man who is coaching you spiritually. You will meet face-to-face with this accountability partner once a week for at least six months. When the six months is up, you will agree to meet with an accountability partner once a week for the rest of your life.
7. You will fully support the kids and me financially during the separation.
8. You will sign a legal document agreeing to a fair and equitable division of our assets and a custody agreement in the event of divorce.

YOUR ABUSER'S REACTION TO YOUR LIST

You and I both know that once your team member presents your list to get you back, your abuser is going to have a reaction. I don't want you to be surprised by it, so here are the top four reactions abusers have to the list of requirements.

Possible Reaction #1

He is outraged by your list and refuses to meet any of your requirements. He says and does all the nasty, abusive things I've already mentioned.

That's no big surprise. That's your answer. He offers no acknowledgment of guilt, no repentance. He has not changed.

One abuser took the time to angrily refute every single item on his wife's list. He sent this email to her:

1. I don't need a therapist, you do! You need to learn how to be a good wife because you are a lousy one! Leaving me proves that.

2. I want a complete history of how you have abused me! And it will be a long history!

3. I'm way ahead of you on this one, sweetheart. I am telling my pastor, my family, and our friends what a rotten, selfish person you are. Thanks for leaving me because that action is making my case!

4. These groups are for losers! Step study? You've stepped on me!

5. How dare you question my spirituality! I'm fine with God. I serve in the church. I help people in the church. It's you who should work on your spirituality!

6. For your information, I already have several guys on my side. They say you are the one at fault!

7. No, I won't. Why should I? You left me! You are on your own financially. I hope you and the kids don't starve.

8. Dream on. I'd never sign such a bogus document. If you want a divorce, get one.

Possible Reaction #2

He agrees to your list and starts to follow it. But he quits. He may go into full-blown attack mode. Or he may say it's not worth the effort, because you obviously want a divorce. Either is your answer. Just as with Possible Reaction #1, your abuser offers no acknowledgment of guilt, no repentance. He has not changed.

One abusive wife tearfully said she'd complete every item on her husband's list. She begged him to be patient while she did the list. But after two weeks, she had a change of heart. Just as she'd done a million times during their marriage, she suddenly switched from a nice, loving wife to a nasty, rejecting wife.

She mailed his list to him shredded into a thousand pieces. She thoughtfully included a list of things my client would have to do to get her back.

I had my client prepared for this type of reaction, so he was ready. He came up with the brilliant idea of shredding her list and mailing the pieces back to her. No note, just the pieces.

"I believe my work with you is done," I told him. "You know how to handle her."

Possible Reaction #3

He tries to negotiate and alter your list. He doesn't want to act on some of your requirements, and he wants to change others. By this he's saying he wants control and leverage. That's your answer. He offers no acknowledgment of guilt, no repentance. He has not changed.

One abuser, who happened to be a salesman, attempted to negotiate his wife's list. He had "concerns" about a number of the items. He felt several of the items (and by several, he meant all of them) were "unfair." He wanted to meet in person to hammer out a new list.

I suggested that my client, through a support team member, give her response: "I have concerns about your concerns about my list. It was your abuse of me that was unfair. I will not meet with you. I will not alter in any way any of my items on the list. Either you do my list or you don't. It's your choice."

Possible Reaction #4

He actually surprises you and faithfully accomplishes every point on your list. He is in the 5 to 8 percent of abusers who genuinely repent and work hard to change. He does not get angry about your list. He doesn't complain about it. He's thrilled that you gave him a list and that he has a chance to win back your heart.

One abuser, in a miraculous turnaround, actually embraced his wife's list and worked hard to complete every item. Her leaving broke him. He was willing to do whatever he had to do to get her back.

This kind of genuine repentance in an abuser is rare. It can happen, but only when the abused spouse leaves and demands change.

IF YOUR ABUSER TRULY REPENTS

Six months after you give him your list, if he's in the process of actively fulfilling all the requirements and his attitude is humble and godly and loving, you can move to the next phase of recovery.

You stay separated, but you enter couple counseling. You choose a Christian therapist. You may choose the counselor who has been working with him, the counselor who has been working with you, or start fresh with a new counselor. He or she must be a marriage specialist and be happily married. You can ask about the therapist's background. You two and the therapist will spend three to five months focusing on the abuse that you've suffered.

The therapist will help you heal from the damage your husband has done to you, and will also help your marriage to heal.

In my book *I Don't Love You Anymore,* I offer a specific, detailed guide for this recovery phase.

As you heal from your husband's abuse, you can begin to spend some time with him. It's appropriate to go on dates, have time with the family, and attend church together. It might seem obvious, but because of the abuse and badly damaged relationship, there must be no sex during this time. Having sex before building a new, solid, loving, Christian marriage is complete interferes with and confuses the process.

If you get through the abuse recovery phase, you two will work with your therapist to build a brand-new marriage. In these marriage sessions, you will cover practicing good and clear communication, handling conflict, learning and meeting each other's real needs, and learning how to show love to the other person. You will spend another three to five months in this phase. Until you build a new marriage, you will *not* move back in together.

My book *I Don't Want a Divorce* provides a specific, detailed guide in this phase of building a new marriage.

At some point in this process, with your therapist's guidance, you'll begin living together again. Each of the three of you must thoroughly discuss and totally agree upon this decision.

PART 6

When Your Abuser Does Not Want to Change

CHAPTER 20

Pursuing the Matthew 18 Process

I'm going to ask you the most obvious question in the world. Can you imagine your abuser genuinely repenting and completing your list of requirements in order to win you back? Is your answer no? That's what I thought it would be. He's an abuser, and most abusers stay abusers until they die.

When he refuses to complete your list, move quickly to fulfill the next two steps of confrontation in the Matthew 18 process.

BACK TO MATTHEW 18

The first step is to ask the support team member who delivered your list, and perhaps one more team member, to confront your abuser. If your abuser will not meet with them in person, they can communicate their message by phone, email, or mailed letter.

Their message is: "You are in serious sin. You have lost your wife, and that is all your fault. This is your one opportunity to repent of your sin of abuse, come back to God, change, and maybe win back your wife. We're asking you to carry out her list."

When he refuses to listen to your "two or three witnesses" (Matt. 18:16), immediately ask your pastor and church leaders to confront your abuser. You have kept these leaders informed of your situation, so they know all about the abuse and your departure. If your abuser is attending a different church from yours at this point, also ask his pastor and church leaders to confront him. If his church leaders don't know about the abuse and your departure, fill them in.

If your abuser will not meet with the church leaders, they can communicate their message to him by phone, email, or mailed letter. Ask these leaders to deliver exactly the same message that your support team delivered. You are, hopefully, now in a church in which the leaders follow Scripture and will confront your abuser.

> *Matthew 18 is clear. Until the sinner repents and changes, you must stay away from him.*

His church leaders may accept their responsibility, follow Scripture, and confront your abuser. Then again, they may not. It's likely they will believe your abuser's lies and try to confront you! To obey the Matthew 18 process, all you're required to do is ask them to confront the sinner.

When your abuser refuses to listen to the church leaders, or they won't confront him, you will follow Matthew 18 and "he is to be to you as a Gentile and a tax collector" (v. 17). What this means is you will shun him and get away from him. You're already doing this, so just keep doing it.

One client who had just completed these Matthew 18 steps said to me:

It was tough finding Christian men to confront my abusive husband. Literally every man I asked to be one of the witnesses said no. Every one. Spineless and weak! Oh well, I asked.

But my pastor did come through! He sent an email to my husband. I felt so supported. My husband responded with a hateful, nasty email, but at least he was confronted.

I feel good that I obeyed Scripture and completed these Matthew 18 steps. My husband has been given every opportunity to repent.

Matthew 18 is clear. Until the sinner repents and changes, you must stay away from him. You will continue to live apart from him and to build your new life.

GET READY FOR WORLD WAR III

After you've presented your abuser with the list of required actions to win you back, chances are he's not merely unrepentant, he's also furious. He's in a rage that comes flowing out of deep insecurities that reside in his core, insecurities that he often compensates for by domineering, by always needing to be right, by never admitting fault, and so on. You've broken his control of you, which is inexcusable to him and leaves him in a position he cannot accept: vulnerable.

To protect his reputation and the façade he has built, and to pay you back for having the gall to leave him, he will go after you with every nasty trick in the book.

One client told me:

He was already furious because I left him. But after I followed the Matthew 18 steps, and the witnesses and church leaders confronted him, he flew into a super rage mode.

He came after me and the kids and my support team with a vengeance. For two solid months, he did everything he could to try to make me suffer and regret leaving him.

Well, with God's power and my support team, I weathered the storm. I know he's not done yet, but I don't care. I do not regret leaving him. I regret not leaving him sooner.

The good news is, you are not the weak and dependent person you used to be. You are significantly stronger: spiritually, emotionally, and financially.

You are not standing alone, either—you have a solid support team. You can financially support yourself and your kids. You have a tough, battle-hardened attorney. You have a pastor and church leaders who understand abuse, who believe you, and who are on your side.

You have a godly, experienced Christian therapist who will help you and the kids deal with all the further abuse your abuser will throw at you.

ENTERING THE POST-ESCAPE PHASE

You're going to face World War III. But you're ready for it. Here are some final instructions as you move into the post-escape phase of the war.

Show No Emotion

Don't let your abuser see any emotion from you. He desperately wants to cause you pain and anguish. He wants a taste of victory, something you must not give him. He *will* cause you pain, disappointment, and sadness. Reliving a bit of what you have endured for so long will bring back miserable memories and feelings. Failing to see him repent and show love will bring great sorrow. But never let him know that.

He'll try to call you so he can rant about how terrible you are and vilify you in any way he chooses. Don't talk to him on the phone. He'll send you long, vicious, rambling emails and texts. Scan them for important information that requires action on your part—such as legal matters, money, the children's schedules—and respond to these pertinent issues only.

> *He'll try his best to drag you into extended dialogues. Don't bite.*

Remain calm, logical, rational, and distant with your abuser. You will vent your emotions to God and your support team. As far as your spouse will know, you are untouched by his words and behavior. You have seen it all before.

Communicate Briefly and Only When Necessary

Praise God for technology! You will rarely talk to your abuser in person or on the phone. Most of your communication with him will be by text and email.

Keep your messages and responses brief and to the point. He'll try his best to drag you into extended dialogues. Don't bite. Ignore his hateful and verbally abusive comments. Show no emotion; just express the facts you need to convey. Do not engage at all in defending yourself or in seeking vindication. This would draw attention away from *his* sinful destructive behavior. You left him *because of his treatment of you.*

Save all his nasty, threatening communications. You may be

able to use these in the legal arena. Be careful with your communications with him because he may try to use these against you.

If he becomes unreasonable and out of control in his communication with you, ask your support team to step in and deal with him. If he acts in this way in conversation, end the conversation—hang up or end the text immediately.

When you have to be in his presence, say nothing and ignore him. Don't greet him. Don't talk except to respond appropriately to questions and/or discussion.

If he threatens you with physical harm, report this to the police so there's a record. If he stalks you, call the police. If he refuses to return the children at the agreed-upon time, call the police.

Lean on Your Support Team

You will continue to need your church, friends, and family. Go to them for a listening ear, advice, and practical help. You may need money. You will need babysitters and help with transporting the kids.

Your attorney will handle all the legal garbage your abuser and his attorney shovel at you. Your Christian therapist can play a huge role in assisting you and the kids in managing your abuser.

Coach Your Kids

Working with your therapist, coach your kids so they'll know how to deal with their abusive father. They need to practice responding to his lies, his attacks on you, his broken promises, his attempts to pump them for information about you, his effort to win them over and get them to live with him full time, and any other manipulative behavior.

Tell your kids not to directly confront their father about his sinful behavior. That will cause him to retaliate against them and do real damage. Rather, it's smarter and safer for them to avoid him, to stay busy with other activities when with him, and to never talk to him about you. Teach your children to come up with short, stock replies to their father's attempts to force them into awkward conversations, such as these simple, conversation-ending statements:

"Okay."
"Fine."
"I don't know."
"I don't want to talk about that."
"Let me think about that."

They can switch the topic so they're talking about him and what he's doing in his life, his work, and his leisure time. He's a narcissist, so he loves talking about himself.

Many abused moms I've worked with have told me that the reason they remain with an abuser is so they don't lose time with their kids. Plus, they hate the idea that their kids will be alone with the abuser.

I tell these moms three things: (1) they're harming their kids by staying with the abuser; (2) even if they have their kids only 50 percent of the time, that's a lot better than the kids being with the abuser full time; (3) pray that God will protect their kids when they're with their dad.

Of course, tell your kids that they can call you or text you at any time when they're with their father. If they're struggling with their dad's behavior and treatment of them, assure them that you're available to talk at all times.

Make it clear to your kids that if Dad is abusing them, they need to call the police. Give them the number to call.

Always Have a Backup Plan

Every time—*every* time—your abuser is supposed to take the kids because you have something planned, have a backup plan. If your abuser cancels at the last minute, have someone lined up who can take the kids for the evening, for the weekend, or for the week. And, believe me, he will cancel plenty of times. He'll do this to shaft you, or because he's selfish and finds an activity that's more fun than being with his kids.

HOW ABOUT DIVORCE?

Many of the abused spouses I've worked with have asked me, "Should I divorce him?" It's a very good question. And I always give the same answer:

> It's not my place to recommend divorce. That's a matter only you and God can talk about, and a decision you must make. I go only as far as recommending separation, because this protects you and the kids, and it provides the best chance to save the marriage—which, of course, God wants, you want, and I want. God will make it clear if He releases you from this marriage.

The truth is, God will use my escape plan and your abuser's reaction to your departure to make it obvious as to whether or not He releases you to get a divorce.

Often, your abuser will make financial and child custody moves that give you no option *but* to file for divorce. Or your abuser will file for divorce.

Many abusers will not file for divorce because they want to appear to be taking the moral high ground. Waiting out their spouses and forcing them to file fits their twisted narrative so they can then tell others, "I did my best to prevent a divorce, but she filed."

If God allows you to file, don't use the collaborative divorce process. It's a waste of time, money, and energy. It works only with a reasonable, non-abusive spouse. You don't have a spouse like that. Rely on your attorney to fight for the best deal you can get. And never, ever use only his attorney to work out a divorce settlement. Always rely on your own attorney, because he or she will fight for you and only you.

> *If God releases you from the marriage, you are on solid ground with Him.*

Listen to me. If you do file, no one on earth who knows you and loves you will have a problem with your decision. And more importantly, I firmly believe God will not have a problem with your decision. If God releases you from the marriage, you are on solid ground with Him. He loves you more than anyone else does, and He knows, more than anyone else, the awful pain you've been enduring for too long.

CHAPTER 21

Get Ready to Leave

I want you to read the words of a client who put my entire escape process into action. She had been out for a year and had come back to thank me and to talk about her experience.

> Dave, I still can't quite believe that I left my husband. I will never forget my first session with you. I was sobbing uncontrollably, telling you there was no way I could ever leave my abusive husband. You kept telling me I could do it, with God's help and your plan.
>
> I didn't believe you. I was so weak, so beaten down by his abuse, so pitiful. Every day was a battle just to survive. But, step by step, I followed your plan. You know all the times I got stuck. I got discouraged. I felt hopeless. But I kept working the plan.
>
> I slowly got emotionally healthy. I began to think that maybe I could leave. Maybe I could support myself and the children. Maybe I could live a new life.

Well, all my *maybes* have turned into *yes, I cans!* I won't lie. Your plan was brutally tough. Incredibly painful. And you know how long it took me to get ready to leave.

But the only thing worse than your plan was staying with my abuser. That would have been far, far worse. Staying would have destroyed me and the kids.

Life isn't easy now. It's hard. Money is tight. It's tough doing everything myself. I still have to deal with the abuser. But I'm a lot stronger. The kids are a lot stronger. We are healthier emotionally, physically, and spiritually.

We're making it! Life is difficult. But life is better. Life is good! God is good. I never dreamed I could say life is good. I'm looking forward to God's plan for me and my children.

How long have you been suffering with your abuser? A year? Five years? Fifteen? Twenty? More?

However long it's been, it's been too long.

It's time to get ready to leave.

The information and advice in this book are a lot to take in. I get that. I also understand that you're not ready to leave now. But you're ready to *get ready* to leave.

I've been very tough on you. I've written some things that have offended you and made you angry. That is by design. What I've said is true, but that's not the only reason I've been tough.

> *Above all, you want a man who will love God and walk with God.*

I want to shake you up. I want to shake you up as never before in your life. The stakes are incredibly high for you and your children!

I'm trying with all my being to save your life and the lives of your children *now*, not after more months, or years, of suffering and damage. I want you to see that *your only option for safety* is to leave your abuser.

YOU WANT A MAN WHO . . .

You want a man who is desperately sorry for what he's done to you and the children. You want a man who, without any excuses, will take complete responsibility for his abusive behavior. You want a man who understands why he abused you.

You want a man who will do the hard work on himself to change. You want a man who will *never* abuse you and the children again. You want a man who will learn to love you the way you need to be loved.

Above all, you want a man who will love God and walk with God.

My plan gives your husband the best opportunity he's ever going to have to become this kind of man.

Don't settle for anything less.

YOU CAN LEAVE

God has a plan for your life, and He doesn't want you to suffer at the hands of an abusive husband. Let me remind you of the Bible's commands to husbands:

- Husbands, love your wives, just as Christ also loved the church and gave Himself up for her. . . . husbands also ought to love their own wives as their own bodies. (Eph. 5:25, 28)

- You husbands must be loving and kind to your wives and not bitter against them nor harsh. (Col. 3:19 TLB)
- You husbands . . . live with your wives in an understanding way . . . so that your prayers will not be hindered. (1 Peter 3:7)

You're living a nightmare that will *never* end as long as you stay with your abusive spouse.

God is talking to you when He says: "'I know the plans that I have for you,' declares the LORD, 'plans for prosperity and not for disaster, to give you a future and a hope'" (Jer. 29:11).

God has good plans for you. God has used my escape plan to help many abused wives leave their abusers. You can be the next one to get out.

God, your heavenly Father, wants you to move from victim to victor. From dependent to independent. From passive to assertive. From no life to a new life.

So, Abigail, I hope and pray you've had enough of your Nabal. Work my steps, and get out.

Additional Resources

Other books by David Clarke:

Married but Lonely: Seven Steps You Can Take with or without Your Spouse's Help, with William G. Clarke

I Don't Want a Divorce: A 90-Day Guide to Saving Your Marriage, with William G. Clarke

What to Do When Your Spouse Says, "I Don't Love You Anymore": An Action Plan to Regain Confidence, Power, and Control

My Spouse Wants Out: How to Get Angry, Fight Back, and Save Your Marriage, with William G. Clarke

I Destroyed My Marriage: How to Win Your Spouse Back, with William G. Clarke

I Didn't Want a Divorce, Now What?: How to Deal with Your Ex and Your Kids, Heal, and Get a Re-set

The Secret to Becoming Soulmates: A Couple's Devotional Journey to Spiritual Intimacy, with William G. Clarke

Kiss Me Like You Mean It: Solomon's Crazy-in-Love How-To Manual

A Marriage After God's Own Heart

Honey, We Need to Talk: Get Honest and Intimate in 10 Essential Areas, with William G. Clarke

Men Are Clams, Women Are Crowbars: The Dos and Don'ts of Getting Your Man to Open Up

Parenting Is Hard, and Then You Die: A Fun but Honest Look at Raising Kids of All Ages Right

I'm Not OK, and Neither Are You: The Six Steps to Emotional Freedom

The Top Ten Most Outrageous Couples of the Bible, with William G. Clarke

To order Dr. Clarke's books, set up an in-person or telephone advice session, schedule a marriage intensive, access his podcast and YouTube channel, or schedule a seminar, go to: davideclarkephd.com.

About the Authors

David E. Clarke, PhD, is a Christian psychologist, speaker, podcaster, YouTuber, and author of fifteen books, including *I Don't Want a Divorce, I Didn't Want a Divorce—Now What?*, and *I'm Not Okay and Neither Are You: The Six Steps to Emotional Freedom*. A graduate of Dallas Theological Seminary and Western Conservative Baptist Seminary in Portland, Oregon, he has been in private practice for more than thirty years. David and his wife, Sandy (The Blonde), live in Tampa, Florida, and have four children and four grandchildren. More grandchildren have been promised.

William G. Clarke, MA, was a marriage and family therapist for more than thirty years. He is a graduate of the University of Southern California and the California Family Study Center, where he earned his master's degree. With his wife, Kathleen, he served with Campus Crusade for Christ (now Cru) for nine years. William is the founder of the Marriage & Family Enrichment Center in Tampa, Florida.

I don't want to go home. I'm afraid he'll do it again. *Is it my fault?*

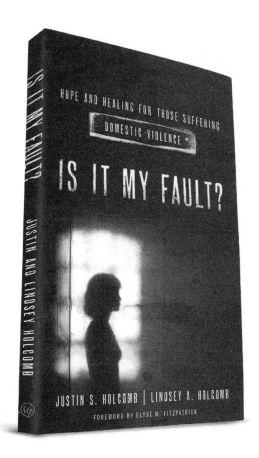

The Healer is inviting you...

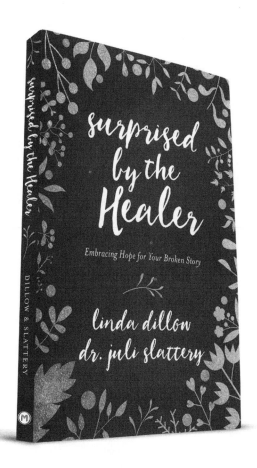

HOW TO FIND FREEDOM TO THRIVE IN RELATIONSHIPS AFTER CHILDHOOD SEXUAL ABUSE

MOODY Publishers

From the Word to Life

As a sexual abuse survivor, Nicole offers women the power and hope necessary to share their story, build intimacy, and develop healthy communication in all their relationships. Also, *Breathe* is a helpful tool for those in a relationship with an abuse survivor by providing guidance, confidence, and encouragement as they seek to provide help and support.

978-0-8024-4865-1 | also available as an eBook